BERGLUND CENTER FOR INTERNET STUDIES

INTERFACE

THE JOURNAL OF EDUCATION COMMUNITY, AND VALUES
Volume 11

Published by
Berglund Center for Internet Studies
bcis.pacificu.edu

Acknowledgements

Published by Staff of Pacific University Oregon's
Berglund Center for Internet Studies,
Forest Grove, Oregon, USA

Jeffrey G. Barlow, Ph. D., Editor
Theresa A. Floyd, Managing Editor
Lilly Huynh, Copy Editor
Jenn Hernandez, Assisting Copy Editor
Jeffrey H. Luong, Publishing Editor
Jeffrey H. Luong, Cover Design
Jenn Hernandez, Cover Design

The on-line version of *Interface* was produced by:
Lilly Huynh, Copy Editor
Jenn Hernandez, Assisting Copy Editor
Kristina Nagai & Patrick Nako, HTML Editors
Ken Hyland & Patrick Nako, Systems Operations

http://bcis.pacificu.edu/interface/

Printed in the United States of America
Volume 11
ISBN 978-0-9834353-1-0 (paperback)
Interface (Forest Grove, Oregon)
ISSN 1940-915X

Berglund Center for Internet Studies
Pacific University
2043 College Way, Forest Grove, OR 97116
http://bcis.pacificu.edu

Acknowledgements

The publication of this annual issue of our journal, *Interface,* volume 11, marks our eleventh year of regular production as an e-journal. It was the generosity of James and Mary Berglund, both alumni of Pacific University, which allowed us to examine the effects of the Internet on individuals and their communities worldwide. We are also grateful to our founding Director, Joe Howell for his support in his role as our Board Chair until late 2011. As Joe's business pursuits have proven increasingly successful in the past several years, Dr. Mark Levitt generously agreed to succeed him as Board Chair.

In addition, we are appreciative to the efforts of our present Program Coordinator, Theresa Floyd, who has brought this volume from virtual to physical reality. Without Theresa's efforts, very little would happen at the Berglund Center!

And of course, we are grateful not only to this year's Berglund Center student staff, but to all the staff members who preceded them for the past decade, many of whom are now employed in the industry or running their own highly successful businesses.

And, of course, we are grateful to our writers and editors, who have made the content enclosed here so useful, informative, and entertaining as it is. We are especially grateful to Jerry Greenfield who has acted as Managing Editor since August 2011, following first my own prolonged medical leave and then my recent retirement.

I have enjoyed a fortunate and varied career involving more than forty years in the classroom, prolonged researching and teaching stints in China, Taiwan, and Vietnam, two Fulbright grants, and appointments at Distinguished Visiting Professor posts at two Chinese Universities and one Vietnamese one. Of all the opportunities, honors and awards that have come to me during those years, none has meant more to me than serving as Director of the Berglund Center, which permitted me to work with our wonderful staff, contributors and editorial board. Thanks colleagues, it was a marvelous voyage which we shared!

Sincerely,

Jeffrey Barlow
Professor Emeritus (Nominee)
Pacific University Oregon
March, 2012

Introduction

Interface, the electronic journal of the Berglund Center for Internet Studies, Pacific University Oregon, is written and produced for those interested in the impact of the Internet on the world around them. The Internet has influenced many aspects of our lives, which include the way we work, communicate, teach, and learn. The utility of the Internet has grown over the years and continues to do so exponentially as people realize the ever-expanding range of its abilities.

At *Interface*, we study all of these phenomena, utilizing the flexibility of an electronic journal, which can be useful to all audience, unlike the rigidly determined form of traditional journals. At the Berglund Center we not only publish the results of our authors' research and thought, but also have the great pleasure of encouraging such productivity through grants and scholarships as well as awards for outstanding articles (chosen by our editorial board).

This volume represents the content of our electronic journal, *Interface*, 2011. This publication includes original work from international scholars, as well as students and faculty of Pacific University. For more information on this project, please see our home page. (http://bcis.pacificu.edu/home)

This is our sixth volume of a fully bound hard-copy publication done under a print-on-demand process. Our first, Yang Desheng's *Jigsaw III* is now available at Amazon [1], as is *Interface*, volume 10, 2010. There you will also find our fully peer-reviewed special volume on the last decade of the Internet, *Internet 2.0, After the Bubble Burst*. We have found this approach useful and practicable, especially for limited edition publications such as this one. This work, too, will soon be available online at all bookstores, including Amazon, and Barnes and Noble*. While our work emphasizes the impact of the Internet, we are also aware of the importance of hard copy publications for such purposes as archival durability, assessment and tenure processes, and simply because as much as we love the Internet, most of us still love a good book. We hope that you will find *Interface* such a book!

Pardon me if I interject a personal note here. As I retired from Pacific University on February first, this will be my last issue of the bound volume of *Interface*. It has been an immense pleasure directing the Berglund Center for the past decade, working with our wonderful student staff, editors, and contributors, and serving you, our loyal audience.

Jeffrey Barlow
Professor Emeritus (Nominee)
Pacific University Oregon

---

[1] *Reference to Amazon and Barnes and Noble throughout this publication implies the on-line retail distributing company and bookseller respectively. Due to Copyright restrictions we were not allowed to use the correct reference.*

Table of Contents

Education – Volume 11 1

Blackboard, Podcasting, and SKYPE, Oh My! Navigating Digital Tools in Teacher Preparation 3

Cyber-School: The Challenges of Teaching and Learning Online From One English Instructor's Perspective 9

Internet 2.0 and the Learning Sciences: The Untold Story of a Timely Historical Meeting 13

Test Taking or Project Building? Internet 2.0 in K-12 Education After the Bubble Burst 17

The Internet Age and Teachers: 2000-2010 29

Two Tin Cans and a String 37

Two Tin Cans and a String: Teaching Liberal Arts Online 41

Gaming – Volume 11 45

Is Runeterra a Website, or Is It a Real Community? 47

'Video Games Are Like Smoking and Lung Cancer' and Other Urban Legends in the Violent Video Game Debate 53

Media – Volume 11 59

The Digital Frontier of Manga Part I 61

The Digital Frontier of Manga Part II 69

The End of Sound Slavery 75

Politics – Volume 11 83

Is Your Business Complying with Website and Email Laws? 85

Social Media – Volume 11 87

Lost in a Crowded Room: A Correlational Study of Facebook & Social Anxiety 89

Social Media: Tool for Social Good or Aid to Slacktivism 95

Technology – Volume 11 101

Barnes & Noble Nook Color: User Review 103

The Internet: Data with a Purpose 109

Kindle Use Abroad 113

Overlays and the Optimal User Experience 117

A Review of the iPad After One Year 123

Book Reviews – Volume 11 127

Dan Breznitz and Michael Murphree, *Run of the Red Queen* 129

Daniel Henrich's Internet Evangelism in the 21st Century 133

Detective/Mystery Fiction and the Impact of the Internet: The Edgar Nominees for 2011 137

Edgar Award Nominees, 2011, and the Impact of the Internet, Part II 145

Jason Ohler's Digital Community: Digital Citizen 155

Robert Glenn Howard's *Digital Jesus* 161

Tim Elmore's. Generation iY: *Our Last Chance to Save Their Future.* 167

Editorials – Volume 11 171

Google's Ngram Viewer 173

Peaceful Evolution in China and the World Wide Web. Part IV: The Internet as the Bulwark of Chinese Democracy? 183

Studying China Online: Editorial Review 193

About the Authors 203

Index 211

Education – Volume 11

Christine Macfarlane - *Blackboard, Podcasting, and SKYPE, Oh My! Navigating Digital Tools in Teacher Preparation*
http://bcis.pacificu.edu/interface/?p=82

Robbie Pock - *Cyber-School: The Challenges of Teaching and Learning Online From One English Instructor's Perspective*
http://bcis.pacificu.edu/interface/?p=320

Mark Szymanski - *Internet 2.0 and the Learning Sciences: The Untold Story of a Timely Historical Meeting*
http://bcis.pacificu.edu/interface/?p=37

Michael Charles - *Test Taking or Project Building? Internet 2.0 in K-12 Education After the Bubble Burst*
http://bcis.pacificu.edu/interface/?p=444

Steve Rhine - *The Internet Age and Teachers: 2000-2010*
http:// http://bcis.pacificu.edu/interface/?p=311

Elizabeth M. Drake-Boyt - *Two Tin Cans and a String*
http://bcis.pacificu.edu/interface/?p=413

Elizabeth M. Drake-Boyt - *Two Tin Cans and a String: Teaching Liberal Arts Online*
http://bcis.pacificu.edu/interface/?p=226

Blackboard, Podcasting, and SKYPE, Oh My! Navigating Digital Tools in Teacher Preparation

Christine Macfarlane

Professor of Education, Pacific University

Just as Dorothy found herself in the strange world of OZ where things did not appear or work like they did in Kansas, teacher preparation candidates enrolled in distance learning, and technology-rich course environments often find themselves lost on the information highway and wondering what to make of OS (operating system). Candidates need a roadmap to facilitate acquisition of course content while utilizing a range of technology tools they may or may not be familiar and/or fluent in using. Similarly, university faculty members need expertise and options for implementing alternative course delivery methods. Distance learning is a necessary part of learning in today's society.

Levels of Elegance

Macfarlane and Smaldino (2000) identified various course delivery models for distance learning and categorized these by level of elegance. Level of elegance is determined by considering whether or not the course is delivered asynchronously or synchronously and sophistication of technology. A low level of elegance would be a correspondence course delivered asynchronously to an individual. A high level of elegance would be achieved if the student participates in a real-time (i.e., synchronous) 2-way audio and 2-way video course with peers. Similarly, a candidate could experience a high level of elegance if he or she participated in an online course via the Internet, whether it was asynchronous or synchronous if the course was developed in an interactive manner.

Just as important is previous experience for instructor and student. It is quite possible that the instructor has never experienced a distance environment as a student. While not a disadvantage as an instructor, it does present a unique set of challenges and certainly can reduce the instructor's comfort level in designing and teaching a distance course. Plus, course content, course outcomes/goals, and instructor style may be harder to deliver or meet within a distance environment. Complicating course development and implementation is the amount of additional lead-time necessary to develop the course along with available tools and experience using technology. Similarly, the student may have no or limited experience as a student in a distance-learning environment along with limited technology experience. Student learning style and choice to take a distance-learning course also have an impact.

Basic Technology Skills

Both instructors and students need basic technology skills to access and utilize (a) a Learning Management System (LMS), (b) institutional library resources, and (c) technology assistance. Additionally, they need Internet search skills along with the ability to download/upload files, send email with attachments, organize electronic files, and use word processing and presentation programs. Further, an open attitude to move beyond their current skill level can be both helpful and empowering.

Generally, a university selects a Learning Management System (LMS) to support faculty development and delivery of course content and student participation. The university may purchase a license and support from a company who provides the LMS to the university (e.g., Blackboard) or the university may choose an open source option such as Moodle. With the open source option, the university has options to adjust and customize the LMS to meet specific needs, styles, and content of instructors, courses, and students. As an instructor you must learn to work within whatever system the university adopts to develop, implement, and manage the course, while as a student, you must learn to participate in the course. Even though a university-sponsored LMS is provided, some instructors choose independently to develop their own website and either to adopt an open-source approach or maintain a closed learning environment. One advantage to an instructor-developed website is students can maintain access beyond enrollment parameters.

Developing the Course

Two important decisions have an impact on the structure and tools needed to deliver a distance-learning course. First, will all students attend class at the same time, or will students participate in class at will? Even though the class may be asynchronous, there can still be timelines for completing modules, topics, or class sessions. Next, will the student interact only with the instructor or will there be student-to-student interaction as well? An instructor has several approaches to providing instruction and engaging the student in course content. She could focus on one approach or build the course using multiple strategies. The simplest approach is a text-based approach; that is, the student reads textbooks, articles, online materials (e.g., e-texts, e-Journals, website publications), and/or teacher-prepared written materials. This approach is similar to an independent study. An instructor can emulate class lectures and present content in the form of webinars, video teleconferencing, podcasts or annotated slide presentations (i.e., written text in the notes section to accompany/expand what appears on the slide). If demonstrations or visual images are critical to learning content, the instructor can incorporate video, graphic images, and/or schedule a face-to-face session. A face-to face session would also facilitate an interactive approach to learning as would discussion or a cooperative learning activity. In all cases, both instructor and student need technology skills along with access to technology tools and software/programs.

Technology for Text

In a text-based approach the instructor might select textbooks, articles and/or online materials. Additionally, the instructor will usually develop written materials. Some students prefer to interact with hard copies or printed versions of text materials. Other students, especially those with disabilities, prefer or need electronic versions. Thus, having both print and electronic options available is extremely useful. In order to provide text materials, an instructor needs word processing and/or publishing software, the ability to create PDFs and/or e-text, and a means by which to embed hyperlinks or share URLs. Embedded hyperlinks insure students reach selected online materials; however, one must maintain some vigilance to avoid link rot. Personally, I have found using a scanner to create an electronic version of certain printed materials an invaluable resource. I also convert all documents to PDFs to maintain consistency across computers, although some file storage options on personal websites may work better with documents.

Several options exist for students to access electronic text-based materials. In addition to, or in lieu of the computer, students might use a multi-purpose hand-held device such as a Smartphone or tablet. An e-Reader is another option. Students also need library privileges and remote access along with Internet access and a printer to produce hard copies. Finally, instructors need similar access, especially so they can preview their materials in a format similar to students. Formative evaluation is a hallmark of quality instruction. Plus, similar access facilitates problem solving when technology glitches occur.

Technology for Presentations

Presentation may occur in a live format through the use of webinars, video technology conferencing (VTC), or face-to-face instruction. Webinars are audio-only, but include the option of sharing the computer screen. That is, the student can view the instructor's computer screen during the webinar. Or, another option is that the instructor and other students can view a selected student's computer screen. Conducting a webinar does require specific software (e.g., AdobeConnect), a microphone, and a willingness on the part of the instructor to learn to use the software.

VTC adds a video component to the presentation. Depending on the VTC system/software the presentation may be point-to-point or point-to-multiple points and be 2-way audio and video or 2-way audio with 1-way video. Again, software is required along with a webcam and microphone. SKYPE, however, is a free option and easy to download. Because the signal is transmitted via the Internet, I have experienced delays between video and audio, a pixilated video, and garbled sound. However, for the most part it has been adequate. I have supervised student teachers at a distance, held office hours, and conducted entire class sessions with students attending class by means of SKYPE. In the process I have discovered it's important to field test the setup ahead of time and have a back-up plan in case the technology fails during the presentation. I have also found it easier if the VTC occurs by means of another computer, especially if I am using my computer as I present to the class.

A hybrid model would include face-to-face instruction. When real-time presentation is not necessary or an option, the instructor can capture a presentation. Options for captured presentations include archived webinars, podcasts, or annotated slides. Podcasts can consist of audio only or audio and video. Video can be real time or digital images. There are a number of ways to create a podcast. You can actually use Microsoft's PowerPoint, a simple digital recorder for audio or video, recording software (e.g., Audacity), or a video application such as Photo Booth to create a podcast. More sophisticated software is specifically available to create or capture a presentation (e.g., ProfCast, Camtasia Relay, GarageBand). The key component to creating a podcast is a good microphone, especially if you are capturing a live presentation. When I create podcasts, quiet space free from noise and distraction is critical.

Once the presentation is captured and uploaded, the student will need a computer or hand-held device (e.g., mp3 player, tablet) and headphones or speakers to view and listen to the podcast. Software/programs such as iTunes or a media player (e.g., QuickTime, Windows Media Player) are also needed. Today's students are so attuned to using these tools to communicate with friends and family that their presence in the classroom is not an issue. Plus, a student can review a podcast as often as needed – something that is not an option in a face-to-face class unless the instructor records the class.

Technology for Demonstrations

Depending on course content and pedagogical considerations, students may benefit from demonstrations. If a face-to-face class session or lab is not an option, then the instructor will need to create or find a demonstration that can be viewed by students. Again, a webinar or VTC might work. However, access to a digital camera and/or digital video recorder along with appropriate software (e.g., iMovie, QuickTime) will facilitate the creation of specific demonstration materials. Other options include utilizing video sites such as YouTube or TeacherTube, streaming videos, on demand videos, or CD/DVDs.

Technology for Interaction

The last instructional option, and perhaps the most exciting in today's society, is an interactive approach. Students often express the need to discuss course content and pedagogically, we know students learn more when actively engaged in learning. Interaction can occur during webinars, VTC, and face-to-face classes. However, a myriad of other tools exist to facilitate instructor-student interaction, instructor-students interaction, and student-student interaction. Instructors can set up discussion boards and require students to respond to questions, read responses, and make comments; hold electronic office hours; create virtual environments (e.g., Second Life); chat, instant message, conference and communicate via telephone and email. Class and group projects can occur in wiki spaces (e.g., GoogleDocs) or other online formats. We can respond to each other by means of text or voice-threads. We can participate in online games or social networking. Earlier in my career I partnered students by phone. Now, I engage with them via SKYPE. Previously, an icebreaker at the beginning of class would occur verbally in real time. A recent class began by having students write about their favorite ice cream in a shared, virtual document.

Implementing the Course

Once materials are ready, the instructor must upload them to the LMS, email materials to students, or provide links to needed websites. Perhaps the biggest stumbling block I discovered is the discrepancy between the name/title of the artifact as it appears within the LMS and the file name when downloaded later to the student's computer. As a result I have found it good practice to reference all materials by their title and electronic file name (e.g., Rubric Examples <rubricexamples.pdf>). Some file names are apparent; others are not. Students, and faculty, who have developed good electronic file organization, will fare far better when it comes to downloading/uploading files, storing and accessing files, and working with the contents of a file. Further, identifying a thoughtful, consistent approach to naming electronic files will assist instructor and student. Student files submitted to an instructor with the student's last name as the initial part of the file name will automatically be alphabetize within an electronic file folder.

Needless to say, developing this kind of class takes more time – time for preparation, implementation, and course delivery. For one thing, you must have access to the Internet to upload and download or view student work and engage in interactive activities. Previously, my worst nightmare, as an instructor, involved a non-working copy machine. Now, there will be glitches, either in the LMS, with personal technology tools, and/or with your students' technology tools. I have found it helpful to include technology requirements on the course syllabus. I also require students to have SKYPE, which I use for electronic office hours or drop-in appointments. SKYPE has a screen sharing option, which I can activate to see what is happening and guide them to a solution.

Teaching is a fairly autonomous act from an instructor perspective. However, there are students in every course. I have found it extremely valuable to solicit their on-going feedback about course structure, materials, and strategies in an effort to fine-tune things throughout the course. My students have found that if I do things consistently, they can adjust and figure out how to navigate the LMS and course requirements. I also have the advantage of seeing all of my students in face-to-face classes. As a result I have been able to gather their feedback, reflect on my own practice, and develop creative and innovative means to deliver courses to students. I have gained confidence in my ability to incorporate new technology without losing sight of pedagogy or content. More importantly, my students have learned the necessary skills and content, vicariously acquired more technology skills, and will hopefully transfer that knowledge and skill into their teaching practice.

Cyber-School: The Challenges of Teaching and Learning Online From One English Instructor's Perspective

Robbie Pock

College of Education Graduate, Pacific University

In a few weeks, an eight-week, online freshman composition course will begin, and I will be teaching it. One of the first assignments my students will complete is a forum post and response discussing their thoughts on traditional versus online classes. I have assigned this forum topic every class for the past five semesters, and the responses are almost always the same. Students consistently say that while traditional face-to-face class formats are "easier" and offer a "better" experience, online classes are more convenient and are often the only way students with full-time jobs, families, or military deployments can pursue a college education.

As an instructor who has taught using a variety of formats ranging from traditional face-to-face to hybrid to fully online, I have to agree with my students. Teaching online has made it possible for me to finish graduate school, homeschool my children, and relocate out of state—all while continuing to teach college level composition and literature; I am grateful for it. But I have to admit that the teaching experience is richer and more enjoyable for me when I am in a room with warm bodies, when I can see their faces, and read their body language. Teaching online, in the absence of any visual contact, and often without any real-time communication, has underscored for me, how important that immediate feedback is. If I can see my students, I can know right away if they are getting the concept of a three-point blueprint, if their attention is drifting, or if they're laughing at my jokes.

Of course the challenges for the online teacher go beyond getting used to interacting with text on the screen instead of faces in a classroom (which, for most of the instructors I know, is one of the biggest reasons they became teachers in the first place). The most immediate difference in terms of actual instruction is that everything the instructor needs to convey to students—from basic class procedures, to how to fix a comma splice—must be either typed or voice recorded. Until I transferred my first class from face-to-face to online, I never realized just how much of my teaching was done by *talking*. Granted, I talk more than the average human, even if you figure teachers (who seem to talk more than ordinary people) into the mix. I had relied heavily on the good-old whiteboard, fast-talking, and lots of emphatic gesturing to instruct my students in the basic elements of composition, and the subtle turns of rhetoric. Teaching online meant I had to somehow accomplish these feats with my hands tied, so to speak, and I found that to be an enormous challenge.

The online student also faces challenges of his or her own. Many of my students, especially those who have not taken an online class before, struggle with self-discipline and time management. Many are newly graduated from a traditional high school setting and are accustomed to lobbying for extensions on late assignments, seeking help at a tutoring center or from a teacher before or after school. Many have had parents, coaches, teachers, and counselors reminding them to keep up with assignments. While it's true that most new college students have to shift from a passive, dependent learning approach to a more pro-active, independent one, based on my observations, this shift is particularly difficult for online students. Since there is no set meeting time, who will know if he doesn't log on to do his coursework for the day? The worst he can expect is an e-mail message or a poor grade, arguably less motivating than a real-life instructor with a grade book in her hand. And when a student has trouble with a concept or assignment, she not only has to take the initiative to seek help and clarification, but she must also articulate what it is she doesn't understand in a written message. In order to do that, she has to know what it is she doesn't understand. That is every bit as difficult as it sounds, especially for a student just learning how to communicate effectively in writing.

After the first few weeks of my first online course, it was unanimous among all parties involved that there were features of traditional face-to-face classes that made learning easier, more efficient, and more enjoyable---features we missed. The first round of essays submitted in that first class made clear that there was a breakdown in the transfer of knowledge somewhere. The question was how could I, as a new online instructor, recreate some of those features in an online format? In addition to beefing up my digital lectures and course documents, I sought the help of the director of the online campus for my community college. Together we set up an online meeting site where my students could log in live and participate in a "web workshop" with me once a week. Since real-time "cyber class" is not part of the paradigm for online classes for our community college, my students were distressed at first by this new requirement, and every semester there are still a few who balk at the idea. The whole point of taking online classes, they argue, is not having to attend class at a set time, whether that means driving to a brick-and-mortar building, or logging on.

The compromise I came up with was that the web workshop would be recorded, and students who could not participate live would be required to view the recording and submit a summary/response. This web workshop element has proven to be a crucial key for me and my students to replicating some of the best things about a traditional class: live interaction, immediate redirection and/or re-teaching of concepts when necessary, and those all-important jokes, though now I have to judge by the tone of their chats whether or not they think I'm funny. I still miss hearing a chuckle ripple through the room, but I've learned to be satisfied with LOL.

There's no denying we live in a digital age, an age where we're willing to do everything online: from banking to dating. There's even a story of a deployed soldier who was by his wife's side as she gave birth, encouraging and weeping and loving her through a live streaming video feed. Surely, we are only just beginning to discover the possibilities of online living and online learning, but as we make our way to those discoveries, it is necessary to reflect and ask questions, to do our best to maintain high standards of teaching and learning. My hope is that this article and many more like it from instructors, administrators, students, and others will contribute to that conversation.

Internet 2.0 and the Learning Sciences: The Untold Story of a Timely Historical Meeting

Mark Szymanski

Associate Professor College of Education, Pacific University

Berglund Fellow

"Explore museums from around the world, discover and view hundreds of artworks at incredible zoom levels, and even create and share your own collection of masterpieces." declares Google. Do this all; right now, for free, on any mobile device, from anywhere in the world at The Google Art Project. [2] How can this be possible? That is a fair question and a multifaceted answer.

The untold story of The Google Art Project has little to do with Google or art, and more to do with the story of the timely meeting of Internet 2.0 and the Learning Sciences and the unplanned reciprocal relationship the two areas have forged with each other during the last decade. The Learning Sciences is an interdisciplinary field of research that seeks to develop a deeper understanding of how we learn in complex and increasingly digital learning environments. [3] The research in the field is influenced by the findings of cognitive science, educational psychology, computer science, and the emerging field of games and learning.

All of these developing understandings are used to improve and design learning environments in the Internet 2.0 era, which are increasingly more rich, complex, and social. To answer the research questions about learning in an Internet 2.0 era, Learning Scientists use a design-based research methodology. This methodology accounts for the characteristics of complex learning systems laden with emergent properties and interactive variables. [4] This allows scientists to account for the robust and dynamic nature of learning in complex environments that provide learners with the immediate ability to store, create, and disseminate knowledge.

As Michael Wesch, a Professor of Anthropology who explores the effects of new media on society and culture, points out.

---

[2] Found at: http://www.googleartproject.com/

[3] Found at: http://www.isls.org/index.html

[4] Brown, A.L. (1992). Design experiments: Theoretical and methodological challenges in creating complex interventions in classroom settings. *The Journal of the Learning Sciences,* 2(2), 141-178.

There is something in the air, and it is nothing less than the digital artifacts of over one billion people and computers networked together collectively producing over 2,000 gigabytes of new information per second. While most of our classrooms were built under the assumption that information is scarce and hard to find, nearly the entire body of human knowledge now flows through and around these rooms in one form or another, ready to be accessed by laptops, cellphones, and iPods. Classrooms built to re-enforce the top-down authoritative knowledge of the teacher are now enveloped by a cloud of ubiquitous digital information where knowledge is made, not found, and authority is continuously negotiated through discussion and participation. [5]

During the Internet 1.0 era, this developing rich cloud of ubiquitous digital information was gathering strength and substance while floating above a landscape ill-equipped to leverage its potential learning opportunities. During the Internet 2.0 era, conceptual and technological advances changed all of this. The Internet, a powerful network, became a participation platform. Rich Internet applications like Flash and Ajax, provided the technical changes necessary to bring desktop experiences to the browsers. Service oriented architecture provided the ability to develop Feeds, Real Simple Syndication, and Mash-Ups. As a result, we have been able to develop web applications that allow learners to access, share, interpret, and design user-generated content as producers and consumers in virtual communities.

Despite the way this has changed how people learn in informal and formal environments, there have been a wide variety of physical, social, and cognitive structures working against the forces of learning in the Internet 2.0 era. "Our physical structures were built prior to an age of infinite information, our social structures formed to serve different purposes than those needed now, and the cognitive structures we have developed along the way now struggle to grapple with the emerging possibilities." [4]

While many of these old physical, social, and cognitive structures stand in the way of rapid change, many new structures are being built to accommodate these changes. In schools, new physical structures are being created, new social structures are being formed, and new cognitive structures are being developed to accommodate learning in this cloud of information. At universities, lecterns and theatre seating are being replaced with networks and modifiable workspaces to support physical and virtual meetings, and in k-12 schools, papers, pencils, and books are being replaced by laptops, tablets, and information clouds.

The new social structures also reflect this change. In addition, the new physical structures, social structures are being built to accommodate the growth of user-

[5] http://www.academiccommons.org/commons/essay/knowledgable-knowledge-able

generated content and social media, blogs, microblogs, wikis, folksonomies, and web applications. These social structures, combined with free digital content storage and distribution services like YouTube, have provided consumers and producers with new social knowledge construction spaces and networks that force us to reconsider the traditional learning paradigms based on print and teacher-directed learning. [6]

The new cognitive structures also reflect this change. The new physical and social structures of learning are pushing educators and Learning Scientists to re-conceptualize old cognitive learning frameworks and strategies and apply them to learning in an Internet 2.0 era. Cognitive strategies that were developed for the physical structures of lecture halls and classrooms, and the social structures of face-to-face communication and interacting with print are being modified to reflect learning in an Internet 2.0 era.

As a result, the changes to the ways we learn have been rapid and unmatched in the history of information and knowledge, and our understanding of how to change is being guided by our developing understandings of the Learning Sciences and Internet 2.0. Learning Science brings the role of the learner and educator into a new place and poses the wonderful question of: What is possible? Anything is possible. Even the ability to "Explore museums from around the world, discover and view hundreds of artworks at incredible zoom levels, and even create and share your own collection of masterpieces."

The Google Art Project has taken museum art from practical obscurity to ambient findability. [7] It is an example of valuing and understanding the important and useful elements of old learning structures and porting those into the new physical, social, and cognitive structures. Doing all of this effectively for other projects and learning opportunities depends on understanding in a detailed and structured way how we learn in an Internet 2.0 environment. Now that we have access to the world's knowledge, it raises the broader question: What does it mean to be knowledgeable? It means moving from being knowledgeable to knowledge-able. [4] Educators are becoming knowledge brokers and learning mentors, using and creating the new physical, social, and cognitive frameworks to guide learners along a path to develop deeper and more complex understandings of what they are learning.

---

[6] Michael Wesch, "A Vision of Students Today (and what Teachers Must Do)," *Encyclopædia Britannica* blog, Oct. 21, 2008, http://www.britannica.com/blogs/2008/10/a-vision-of-students-today-what-teachers-must-do/

[7] http://punya.educ.msu.edu/2008/11/21/we-feel-fine-about-ambient-findability-really/

Test Taking or Project Building? Internet 2.0 in K-12 Education After the Bubble Burst

Michael Charles

Professor of Education, Pacific University

Table of Contents:

Introduction
Technology for testing
Web 2.0 projects
Putting together the total package
What might the future be?

Introduction

At the beginning of the 21st Century, a high school teacher in New Jersey named Will Richardson started reading the book *Secret Life of Bees* [1] with his junior and senior students (Richardson 2010 p. 23). [2] It was a relatively new book, and so he suggested to his students that they use an emerging media tool, a weblog (or blog) to create an online reader's guide to the book. As part of the experience he asked Sue Monk Kidd, the author of the book, to ask if she would join the students in their study of the book. So as his students read the book and began commenting on it, Sue read along with them and began responding to a series of questions they asked. One of her responses ran 2300 words. In Will's classroom a blog was not something you heard about in the news, but something you used both to engage your own learning and to reach beyond the proverbial walls of the classroom. Internet 2.0, the read/write web (often referred to as Web 2.0), was beginning to make the kind of impact in K-12 education that some had imagined.

What happened in K-12 education with the advent of the Web 2.0, after the dotcom bubble burst? After rapid expansion at the end of the 20th Century, the story of the decade, from 2000-2010 involved maturing ways of using the Internet. This article attempts to describe what that maturing use looked like in K-12 education, both in what was hoped for, and what took place. It does so by

---

[1] *Secret Life of Bees* (2002) Retrieved from: http://weblogs.hcrhs.k12.nj.us/bees/ (Note: This Link is no longer valid as the site has been taken down, but you can find more by googling "Will Richardson *Secret Life of Bees*")

[2] Richardson, W. and Mancabelli, R. (in press 2011). *Personal Learning Networks: Using the Power of Connections to Transform Education.* Solution Tree

taking a look back at previous work the author has written in *Interface* and following up on its progress through the lens of Web 2.0 tools.

On the whole, it appears that despite the availability of increasingly easier to use Web 2.0 tools such as wikis, blogs, and podcasts, the past ten years has seen a marked decline in the kind of project-based learning with technology in K-12 schools that is exemplified by Will Richardson's students' work as described above. Instead, the Internet is being used increasingly, to more efficiently measure student achievement on a school wide basis, which is part of a production mindset that is pervasive in the culture as a whole and enjoys increasing influence in education in particular. This movement has been counterpointed by the limited use of Web 2.0 tools to reach the worldwide audience promised by the Web and encountered by Will Richardson's students. In addition there has been an increase in the sophistication of the models used to describe exemplary technology use in schools as combining new technology, progressive pedagogy, and knowledge of content for curriculum-based planning by educators. In the end one hopes that the next ten years will see the re-emergence of more project-based work, although the outlook for change in that direction is not particularly promising at present.

Technology for Testing

In the past ten years the Internet has moved into mainstream use in K-12 education across the United States. [3] The widespread use of Web 2.0 applications mean that authoring on the web requires a very accessible set of skills for the general population: if a user can write an email and attach a file, that user can author and collaborate on the Web. The combination of easier to use tools and widespread access in the schools has led to maturing uses of the web in K-12 schools. But has maturing use in K-12 schools in the past ten years meant better use?

Earlier in the decade the argument was made in *Interface* about how technological thinking holds the threat of reducing education from a cultural task to a production task. [4] The cell phone that has become the ubiquitous technological object of the 21st Century is a perfect example of the triumph of technical thinking. Imagine comparing a cell phone from 2000 and a cell phone from 2010. Both phones transfer digital information wirelessly from an expanding number of locations around the globe. What is the difference between

---

[3] DeBell, M., and Chapman, C. (2006). "Computer and Internet Use by Students in 2003" (NCES 2006-065). U.S. Department of Education. Washington, DC: National Center for Education Statistics.

[4] "Charles, M. (2007). "Where Are We Going As We Leave No Child Behind? La Technique and Postman, Papert, and Palmer-Part Three." *Interface: the Journal of Education, Community, and Values*; v 7 no. 3 retrieved from http://bcis.pacificu.edu/journal/article.php?id=194.

the two, and why is the newer phone perceived to be better? The newer phone does the same task faster, more efficiently, and more cheaply; that is the essential set of values of the technical mindset. Because of that, one can interact with the newer phone differently (a touch screen instead of a microphone and a speaker for voice). Today's cell phones are described in the parlance of the day as simply amazing, but at the most fundamental level, they are quite predictable. They do the same thing cheaper, more efficiently, and faster as their predecessors and thus they are able to provide new capabilities (e.g. streaming video over the Internet). Technical thinking, whose basic ethic is greater efficiency of systems, is invaluable in perfecting production tasks such as the making of a cell phone. But technical thinking has serious flaws when it comes to cultural tasks, whose means and ends are considerably more complex than simple production tasks. [5]

The first piece of legislation passed by the George W. Bush administration with a bipartisan consensus before the events of September 11, 2001 was the reauthorization of the Elementary and Secondary Education Act (ESEA), frequently referred to as No Child Left Behind (NCLB) 2001. NCLB represented a watershed mark in a century-long movement to think of education as a production task. Standards are established for all students—analogous to a set of product specifications for a production assembly line. Curricula are written for teachers to use to build those products. Standardized examinations function as quality control checks of those products on that production line. NCLB mandates that all products from the line be raised to a certain quality standard—i.e. all students must pass the exam (no child should be left behind). It is difficult to argue against this notion of higher quality, especially when one views education as a production task. [6]

The first major piece of legislation offered by the Obama administration, related to K-12 education, is funding for the Race to the Top. [7] It carries production level thinking to the next step, awarding funds to states so that they may pilot different ways of rewarding teachers based on measures of their productivity. Thus as described above, standards have been set, measurements (student achievement scores) have been put in place to check for productivity of the system, and now compensation to workers will be based on increases in agreed

---

[5] B Charles, M. (2004). "Where Are We Going As We Leave No Child Behind? La Technique and Postman, Papert, and Palmer-Part Two." *Interface: the Journal of Education, Community, and Values.* April/May 2004; v 3 no. 4 retrieved from http://bcis.pacificu.edu/journal/2004/03/charles.php.

[6] A Charles, M. (2004). "Where Are We Going As We Leave No Child Behind? La Technique and Postman, Papert, and Palmer-Part One." Interface: the Journal of Education, Community, and Values. February 2004; v 4 no. 1 retrieved from http://bcis.pacificu.edu/journal/2004/01/charles.php

[7] "Race to the Top: Oregon School Leaders Lacking Needed Energy, Drive." http://tinyurl.com/ORRace2TheTop

upon measures of productivity. Typically those measures are improved student achievement scores and perhaps including some form of classroom observation in the assessment of the teacher. [8]

Thus the first ten years of the 21st Century have seen the continued extension of technical thinking on a bipartisan basis into the field of education. The major shift in the use of technology in K-12 schools through the decade has been in the use of technology as part of a comprehensive assessment tool in a production system instead of the anticipated incorporation of Web 2.0 tools for student projects. Internet connected computer labs and classroom sets of laptop computers on carts are consistently used for administering state tests at schools around the country, with results being reported to central data systems served via the Web. This means that those same computer resources are not available for students to use to employ Web 2.0 tools for projects.

Web 2.0 Projects—What Could Be

As noted at the beginning of this article, one of the big stories of the past ten years was the emergence of Web 2.0 tools like weblogs or blogs. Will Richardson, sometimes described as "the blog evangelist," has written in great detail about how Web 2.0 tools can change education, providing the kinds of tools that allow a teacher to shift their role from the proverbial "sage on stage" to a "guide alongside" of students as they learn.

In the soon to be released *Personal Learning Networks,* Will Richardson and Rob Mancabelli take a visit to another teachers' classroom to see how the web could be used to allow students to reach beyond the classroom and become learners connected to the 21st Century world:

> *"Seventh and eighth grade teacher Clarence Fisher has an interesting way of describing his classroom up in Snow Lake, Manitoba. As he tells it, it has "thin walls," meaning that despite being eight hours north of the nearest metropolitan airport, his students are getting out into the world on a regular basis, using the Web to connect and collaborate with students in far flung places from around the globe. The name of Clarence's blog, "Remote Access," sums up nicely the opportunities that his students have in their networked classroom.*
>
> *Learning is only as powerful as the network it occurs in," Clarence says. "No doubt, there is still value in the learning that occurs between teachers and students in classrooms. But the power of that learning is more solid and*

---

[8] Associated Press, 2011. "Beyond Pass-fail: Washington Considers More Specific Teacher Evaluations." Retrieved from: http://tinyurl.com/ByondPassFail

more relevant at the end of the day if the networks and the connections are larger."

Without question, Clarence imbues the notion of the "connected learner." Aside from reflecting on his life and his practice on his blog, he uses Twitter to grow his network, uses Delicious to capture and share bookmarks, and makes other tools like Skype and YouTube a regular part of his learning life. In other words, he's deeply rooted in the learning networks he advocates for his students.

It's changed everything for me as a learner," he says. "I teach in a small school of 145 v, so I don't know what it's like to have a lot of colleagues. I can't imagine closing my door and having to generate all of these ideas on my own." [9]

This is the Web 2.0 that so many imagined. It is a tool for going public with student work, and a way for a teacher to connect with other like-minded educators to develop further as a professional. As we continue into the 21st Century, the number of tools and their availability seems to only be proliferating. These tools are profoundly decentralized, in that Clarence is constructing his own personal program of professional development [10] and using the Internet to do it.

This same Web 2.0 has great promise for students. I have written about Silas, a 4th grade student in a relatively lower SES school in New Zealand and the way that he uses his blog and related multimedia tools to publish his work to the world. [11] Here I summarize some of those same points in reference to the larger trends discussed in this article. Silas' entry "My waka animation adventure" was one of the first things that he wrote after only two weeks in 4th grade learning about how the Polynesians had migrated from one island to the next in the Pacific aboard giant double sailing canoes called *waka*. He created a computer-animated drawing that showed what he learned, and that animated drawing was published as an entry on his blog that he narrated:

"While the waka was battling the odds, the numerous stormy and rough waves were crashing over them. The people were frightened and sad as waves crashed over the waka. And the fierce wind howled like a wolf's cry."

---

[9] Richardson, W. and Mancabelli, R. (in press 2011). *Personal Learning Networks: Using the Power of Connections to Transform Education*. Solution Tree

[10] Charles, M. & Kolvoord, R.A. (2011). "Geospatial Semester: Developing Students' 21st Century Thinking Skills with GIS." Proceedings of the American Educational Research Association.

[11] Charles, M., Burt, D., Williams, M.K. (2010/2011) "Lessons from New Zealand: Developing students' voices using technology." *Learning and Leading with Technology*, December/January 2010/2011 (Volume 38, number 4)

The energy in Silas' writing is palpable, and his work suggests that he might comprehend at a rather personal level at least some of the dangers of this most hazardous journey of the Maori.

Silas kept his blog throughout the school year essentially as a learning journal, similar to what many educators have envisioned blogs would be used effectively in classrooms. [12] He made over 20 blog entries (about two or three posts per month). The topics he posted on ranged from things he was learning in school (like the waka adventure, volcanoes, and using descriptive words) to things he loves to do (like his Michael Jackson moonwalk). Silas' classroom only has a few computers in it that students successfully share. There is no lab of computers to visit, nor a cart of laptops for every student to use. Internet access in his school is at a slower rate than at many schools in the United States. The educators that lead his school have plans underway to provide greater high-speed access to computers in his school, but it is not for the purpose of administering standard assessments of student achievement, but instead as a tool for more students to go public with their work.

Draw and talk about what you are learning is a simple and fundamentally sound educational strategy, especially for students at the elementary school level. Having students post on their own blogs for a larger world to read and comment on is an idea that many advocate (Richardson, 2010) [13] but a relatively small percentage of students in the US actually do, often because of safety concerns. Yet at Pt England School in New Zealand, the public school where Silas attends, those safety concerns are balanced by the conviction that student voices need to be heard, and that publishing to the web is a critical part of developing students as confident, connected, and actively involved lifelong learners. Silas' blog and those of his classmates are open to the world so that any one can read and comment on them. Many of the readers are students from the school or family members of the writers, but a quick look at the map on the blog shows that readers come from several continents. [14]

In 2000 the kind of use for these emerging Web 2.0 tools that many in the US envisioned was similar to what has been described above for Clarence as a teacher and for Silas as a student. But particularly in the United States, Internet use has instead been focused on using this technology as part of a comprehensive assessment system whose intent is to measure the productivity

---

[12] Bull, G., Bull, G., & Kajder, S. (2003). "Mining the Internet - Writing with Weblogs." *Learning and Leading with Technology*. 31 (2): 32-35.

[13] Richardson, W. and Mancabelli, R. (in press 2011). *Personal Learning Networks: Using the Power of Connections to Transform Education*. Solution Tree

[14] Pt England School

Pt England School site: http://www.ptengland.school.nz/

Pt England School blogs: http://www.ptengland.school.nz/index.php?family=1,451

Pt England School—Silas' blog: http://pessilasd.blogspot.com/

of students and teachers in K-12 schools. This move from project-based learning with technology to the more efficient use of these tools for measuring student achievement is part of a system-wide focus on raising test scores. What is being lost in this effort? Alfie Kohn suggests that "we should worry because of what schools are sacrificing in order to focus on raising test scores: recess, music and the arts, inquiry-based science, the time to read good books, interdisciplinary projects, class meetings, field trips, discussion of current events – the list goes on and on. [15] One can add project-based computer learning to this list of things being lost in schools in the USA.

Putting Together the Total Package

One of the encouraging trends in Internet use in education in the past ten years is the increasingly sophisticated way in which technology and content have been connected. For many years those who use technology in the schools have made the point that the question is not really about technology, but about learning. [16] To ask how one might use a particular set of technologies, such as Web 2.0 tools, in the schools is to frame the question incorrectly. It is an example of what has been described as technocentric thinking [17] when what really needs to be considered are educentric applications of Internet 2.0 tools in education. Richardson's discussion of the use of wikis, blogs, and podcasts earlier in this article is a good example of this notion. The idea is that the technology is essentially invisible, and the focus is on the learning. The power of Silas' blog is not that he is writing a blog, but that he is writing for a larger audience, using the Internet.

This idea of how to effectively put together technology, content, and pedagogy has been more succinctly described in the past ten years with the TPACK (Technology, Pedagogy, and Content Knowledge) model. TPACK has been defined as:

> *"Technological Pedagogical Content Knowledge (TPACK) attempts to capture some of the essential qualities of knowledge required by teachers for technology integration in their teaching, while addressing the complex, multifaceted and situated nature of teacher knowledge. At the heart of the*

---

[15] Kohn, A. (2002-03). The Worst Kind of Cheating. *Streamlined Seminar--a publication of the National Association of Elementary School Principals.*

[16] Russell, Anne L. (1995). "Stages in Learning New Technology: Naive Adult Email Users," *Computers & Education*, (Volume 25, Issue 4), pp. 173-178, retrieved from http://tinyurl.com/AdultEmailUsers

[17] Papert, S. (1987). "Computer Criticism vs. Technocentric Thinking." *Educational Researcher* (vol. 16, no. I) retrieved from http://www.papert.org/articles/ComputerCriticismVsTechnocentric.html

TPACK framework, is the complex interplay of three primary forms of knowledge: Content (CK), Pedagogy (PK), and Technology (TK)." [18]

The key idea is that in order to use technology to create better learning opportunities for students, teachers must know their content, know how to teach (pedagogy), and know the affordances that emerging technologies provide. At the intersection of these three forms of knowledge is the "sweet spot" of effective technology use in schools, or TPACK. In an article written earlier this decade [19] this idea was referred to as putting together the total package. To really use these Web 2.0 tools effectively, a teacher needs to first draw on strong content knowledge and pedagogical knowledge in combination with technological knowledge. In the first 10 years of the 21st Century, what distinguishes the technological tools is that they are generally getting easier to use. But that does not insure better educational outcomes because the difficulty is not how to use the technology. The challenge is to put together the total package.

This TPACK model has been well defined in the educational research community as a construct for taking a more thoughtful look at what has previously been called technology integration. As one source stated:

"Advances in technology combined with widespread user participation clearly create opportunities in education that did not exist previously. We can assist teachers in reflecting, planning, and enacting instructional strategies based on the TPACK intersection." [20]

The TPACK model may be an important part of allowing technology to realize greater potential in the schools for the paradoxical reason that it broadens the conversation beyond technology, into content, and pedagogy.

Other serious efforts at charting the intersection of technology, pedagogy, and content knowledge are underway in conversations about the importance of quality professional development for teachers. [21] The failure of previous efforts is described as that it is often focused on learning the new technology. The real problem is putting technology, pedagogy, and content together. Curriculum-based educational technology professional development for teachers is an idea

---

[18] TPACK website retrieved from http://www.tpack.org/tpck/index.php?title=Main_Page

[19] Borthwick, A., Charles, M., Pierson, M., Thompson, A., Park, J., Searson, M., Bull, G. (2008). "Realizing Technology Potential through TPACK." *Learning and Leading with Technology*. 36(2): 23-26

[20] Borthwick, A., Charles, M., Pierson, M., Thompson, A., Park, J., Searson, M., Bull, G. (2008). Realizing Technology Potential through TPACK. *Learning and Leading with Technology*. 36(2): 23-26

[21] Harris, J. (2008). "One Size Doesn't Fit All: Customizing Educational Technology Professional Development. Part One: Choosing ETPD Goals." *Learning & Leading with Technology*, 35, 5, 18.

that has been advanced to help guide future efforts in the schools so that as millions are spent on technology infrastructure, teachers are better able to use these resources as part of a total package to improve learning . [22]

Thus if the Internet technology in use in the schools today can be freed up from the fiction that it can be used to increase educational productivity and is instead used to unleash student learning, then the TPACK model can help us move beyond the hype that the Internet will revolutionize education and on to more serious discussions of learning. TPACK and better professional development for teachers are important ideas that have developed in the past 10 years of discussions that might lead the way.

---

[22] Hofer, M. & Harris, J. (2009). "LEARNING CONNECTIONS - Social Studies - Tech Integration in Social Studies." *Learning and Leading with Technology*, 37, 2, 26.

What Might the Future Be?

Over the past 30 years, critiques of secondary education have called for greater rigor in high school courses. [23] The proliferation of Advanced Placement (AP) courses in high schools across the nation has been one response to these calls. AP courses enrolled 3.2 million students in 2010. [24] These courses offer greater rigor as assessed by a standardized examination, which students may opt to take for college credit for a fee. Yet there is no personal higher education involvement in these courses. Recent research suggests that merely taking AP courses is not a valid indicator of eventual college success. [25] The idea behind the AP system is one based on notions of productivity—students enroll in the same courses in high school that they would take in college—has been described as "learning the same stuff sooner." [26] Defining better high school courses as learning the same stuff sooner is an extension of the kind of productivity thinking described earlier in this article.

There is a different definition of more rigorous high school courses that accompanies much of the "school reform" discussion. [27] There have been many calls for the need to teach 21st Century Thinking Skills for high school students. [28] This might be called "learning different stuff deeper." To that end there is a

---

[23] National Commission on Excellence in Education. (1983). "A Nation at Risk: The Imperative for Educational Reform." Washington, DC: U.S. Department of Education.

[24] Kramer, B. (2011). Lake County Part of National Upswing in High-test Academics. *Chicago Sun Times.* Retrieved at: http://tinyurl.com/LakeCountyAcademics.

[25] Geiser, Saul, & Santelices, Veronica. (2004). "The Role of Advanced Placement and Honors Courses in College Admissions." UC Berkeley: Center for Studies in Higher Education. Retrieved from: http://escholarship.org/uc/item/3ft1g8rz.

[26] Charles, M. & Kolvoord, R.A. (2004). "Using Visualization Tools for Inquiry-Based Science: A Longitudinal Study of Teacher's Stages of Development." Research Paper/Roundtable paper at the National Educational Computing Conference of the International Society for Technology in Education (ISTE).

[27] Tyack, D. B., & Cuban, L. (1995). *Tinkering toward utopia: A century of public school reform.* Cambridge, Mass: Harvard University Press.

[28] *21st Century Skills*

Assessment and Teaching of 21st Century Skills. (2009). Retrieved from http://www.atc21s.org/white-papers/.

The enGauge 21st Century Skills Continua of Progress. (2003). Retrieved from http://www.metiri.com/features.html.

Lemke, C. (2003). "enGauge 21st Century Skills: Digital literacies for a Digital Age." Retrieved from http://www.metiri.com/features.html. (ERIC Document Reproduction Service No. ED463753).

The Partnership for 21st Century Skills. (2004). Retrieved from http://www.p21.org/

course being offered at a significant number of high schools in Virginia called the Geospatial Semester (GSS). [29] In this semester or year-long course, high school students learn about geospatial technologies such as Geographic Information Systems (GIS), Global Positioning Systems (GPS), and Remote Sensing. They then apply this new technical knowledge to a local community based problem as the capstone project for the course. They may earn dual credit from a Virginia university in a course that is taught by a local high school teacher who is capable in the use of these tools. Higher education faculty who visit classrooms regularly as well as offering email support provide project mentoring and technical support for the course.

GSS has been underway for the past 5 years and nearly 1000 students have completed the course. In the 2009-2010 academic year the course was offered in 15 different high schools and in a total of 20 different classes in 10 different school districts. Thus while this is not a nationwide innovation, it is at least being carried out on a scale of multiple school districts that holds promise for broader implementation. Typical projects include an assessment of the risk of fire for properties adjacent to the Shenandoah National Park. The student devised a rubric that integrated a number of factors, including proximity to forest, type of forest and amount of open terrain to develop a rating system and then displayed the differential risk on a series of maps of the properties. Another project done by a pair of students was an assessment of the traffic pattern of a Northern Virginia high school. The students took data for traffic, pedestrian, and parking patterns at a variety of times before and after school, analyzed the data and developed a set of solutions and supporting maps to try to alleviate congestion.

These are the kind of projects that the Internet can help make possible in our schools, both as a source for data for projects and for project publication. The curriculum-based professional development necessary to allow teacher to teach the GSS course relies on high quality professional development experiences for teachers. [30] To support their work with their students, teachers need online resources and communication tools—all part of a 21st Century workplace envisioned by many authors in *Interface* and other publications. The possibility of building and sustaining meaningful communities of professional practice using the Internet to support the teaching of courses like Geospatial Semester is most promising. Project-based work might emerge triumphant in the next ten years as the Internet continues to develop. But as long as productivity thinking

---

21st Century Workforce Commission-National Alliance of Business (June 2000). Building America's 21st Century Workforce. Executive Summary, page 5.
Cited in Twenty-First Century Skills. Retrieved from http://www.metiri.com/features.html

[29] Geospatial semester website http://www.isat.jmu.edu/geospatialsemester/.

[30] Kolvoord, R.A., Charles, M., & Purcell, S. (manuscript accepted for publication in 2010). "What Happens After the Professional Development: Case Studies on Implementing GIS in the Classroom." In MaKinster, J., Trautman, N., Barnett, M. (Eds.), *Teaching Science and Investigating Environmental Issues with Geospatial Technology.* New York: Springer Publishing

continues to emerge and dominate the educational landscape, the Internet will be to be used as a more efficient tool for measuring a very confined definition of student learning called student achievement scores. The question is should the Web be used for test taking or project building?

The Internet Age and Teachers: 2000-2010

Steve Rhine
Willamette University

> "I am entirely certain that twenty years from now
> we will look back at education as it is practiced in most schools today
> and wonder that we could have tolerated anything so primitive."
>
> *John W. Gardner, Secretary of Health, Education, and Welfare, 1968*

Clarions marking the demise of traditional K-12 education have repeatedly been heard over the years. Technological advances are usually the motivating culprit. Edison (1922) wrote that "the motion picture is destined to revolutionize our educational system and that in a few years it will supplant largely, if not entirely, the use of textbooks." Needless to say, history said otherwise. From televisions to VCR's to computers to handheld devices, the promise of a new age in education always seems to disappoint in the end. Cuban (1986) describes a cycle that is often repeated in the quest for change in education through technology: "exhilaration/scientific credibility/disappointment/teacher-bashing" (p. 5). The status quo is a powerful force. We develop comfort with our practices and institutionalize policies and attitudes that ensure a stable and predictable future. At the beginning of the decade there were great hopes that the Internet would be a place in which learners could interact and share knowledge as a way to transform the educational process (Kozma & Schank, 1998). Has the rise of the Internet changed K-12 education?

When we look at the number of computers in classrooms over the past 20 years, we can see a dramatic change in the quantity of technology available to teachers and students. Since the first inkling that computers might have a role in classrooms, businesses have been keen on getting schools to devote a bigger and bigger portion of their budgets to technology. Apple began the charge by donating thousands of computers to schools in the 1980's in the hope that students would become accustomed to using Macintosh computers and their parents would buy them at home. Over time, Apple became less philanthropic and schools purchased the cheaper Windows machines instead. $70 billion was spent on school technology in the 1990's (Oppenheimer, 2004). In the end, there is now an average of 1 computer for class use for every 3.1 students (Nagel, 2010) while there was 1 computer per 20 students at the start of the 1990's (Kim & Bagaka, 2005). We have gone from 84% of teachers having at least one computer in their classrooms at the beginning of this decade (NCES, 2000) to

97% of teachers by the end (Gray, Thomas, Lewis, & Tice, 2010). We have poured massive amounts of money into schools to make technology/the Internet accessible to students and teachers.

Of course, the biggest question is whether we have accomplished anything with that investment. Access is certainly not the same as a productive and effective use that ultimately increases learning. Accordingly, answering that question is a multilayered process.

- How has access to the Internet changed in the past decade?
- How has the Internet changed teaching?
- How has the Internet changed learning?
- What are the implications for education for the future?

As one peels through each layer, the issue of the digital divide is raised as well. In the following, I examine the first two layers and how or whether change has come to school via the Internet. I elaborate on all of these layers and discuss the digital divide and school learning at home in detail in an upcoming book from the Berglund Center.

Access

There has been significant growth in school access to the Internet over the past 15 years (see Figure 1). Beginning with only 3% of schools with Internet access in 1994, essentially every school in the country has access to the Internet in 2011, a phenomenal achievement. At the beginning of the Internet decade, a digital divide in schools existed in regard to number of computers as well as to Internet access. By 2010, the digital divide in school shrank, as 80% of students from families with incomes of $20,000-$24,999 used computers in school compared with 86% of students from families with income of $75,000 or more. In regard to the digital divide in schools now, there is not a significant difference (less than 3%) in the number of computers available between elementary and secondary teachers, city versus rural schools, size of school, or percent of students in school eligible for free or reduced-price lunch programs (Gray, et al., 2010). The Internet decade has seen schools' physical access to the Internet become essentially universal, regardless of socio-economics, with an increasing number of students able to access it in their classrooms.

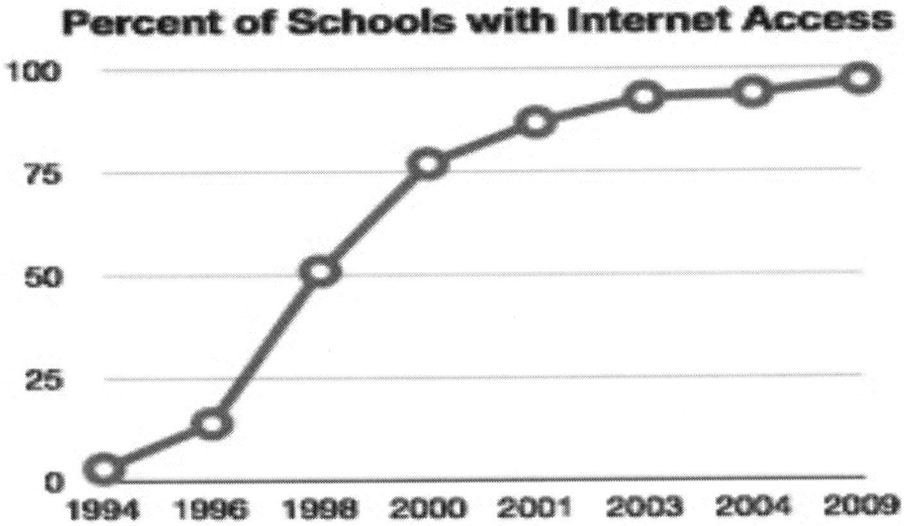

Figure 1 Percent of schools with Internet access (Gray, et al., 2010)

Teachers have access to the Internet. However, for teachers, access is relative. "The physical location and organization of computer technologies, whether the lab, classroom, library, or even school hallway, delimits and shapes the ways which teachers talk about and make use of their schools. As with the distribution of and access to any kind of resource, the distribution and organization of technology has an impact on the frequency and quality of teachers' integration/implementation efforts" (Jenson & Rose, 2008). For example, it matters where the access to the Internet resides. If it is in a library, that leads to one kind of use for teachers. A computer lab implies a distinctive kind of use. A few computers in the classroom create still different ways of potentially using the Internet. Has that access changed teaching?

First, the Internet has fundamentally changed how teachers prepare for their lessons. 94% of teachers 'sometimes' or 'often' use the Internet to prepare for instruction (Gray, et al., 2010). Another element that is growing is the use of the Internet for teacher professional development. In a recent Boston College study of 330 elementary and middle school math and language arts teachers, courses online improved teachers' instructional practices and subject matter knowledge, ultimately facilitating learning gains for students (Cohen & Orne, 2010).

Over the past decade, the Internet has developed into a great networking tool for examining others' syllabi or course plans as well as tapping into state and district resources. In Oregon there is an excellent website created by the Department of Education in which there are searchable state standards as well as examples of assessments and activities tied to those standards. Other states have similar curricular resources. The past decade has seen teachers and states increasingly rely on the Internet to design and access curriculum.

Teachers will likely tell you that the most rewarding and the most challenging aspect of their job is meeting each individual student's needs. There is also a sense that students' physical and emotional well-being has changed over the past decade or two, leaving teachers to cope with a range of student behaviors that were not as prevalent in classrooms previously. In 71% of schools Individual Education Plans (IEPs) are now available through the Internet and 47% of teachers use those IEPs sometimes or often (Gray, et al., 2010). The complexity of issues that students bring with them to school requires teachers to have an understanding of medical/behavioral conditions they previously did not need to consider. Through websites such as WebMD.com, Wikipedia, and social networks, the Internet has become the 'go to' place for teachers to understand the diversity of students' needs in their classroom.
States increasingly rely on the Internet for distribution of state standards and assessment of those standards. Online testing has revolutionized the evaluation of students' understanding of the standards. When testing is managed through the Internet, states and teachers get immediate feedback regarding how well students do on the state tests. Approximately 94% of teachers use their computers for examining test results as well as entering grades and attendance (Gray, et al., 2010). Parents, students, counselors, and administrators can typically have access to that data at any time, facilitating monitoring of students' progress and communication with teachers.

Teachers report that the majority of them are using computers in their classrooms for instruction: 40% often and 29% sometimes (Gray, et al., 2010). However, there was a significant difference between elementary and secondary teachers who reported that they or their students used computers in the classroom during instructional time (74% of elementary teachers, 59% of secondary teachers). Teachers surveyed in the National Center for Education Statistics' study said that their students used technology in a variety of ways, many requiring Internet use (see Figure 3). However, over the past ten Internet years, the web has transformed. In 1999 DiNucci wrote "The first glimmerings of Web 2.0 are beginning to appear...The Web will be understood not as screenfulls of text and graphics, but as a transport mechanism, the ether through which interactivity happens" (p. 32). We have experienced a paradigm shift this decade away from the Internet as a resource to the Internet as interactive. The public has gone from consumers to creators to community. Schools are lagging behind that revolution. Most K-12 teachers have their students make use of Web 1.0 by doing research on the Internet to find information as opposed to using it as a publishing and discussion space, but few teachers had their students contribute to class web pages, blogs, wikis or similar Web 2.0 media.

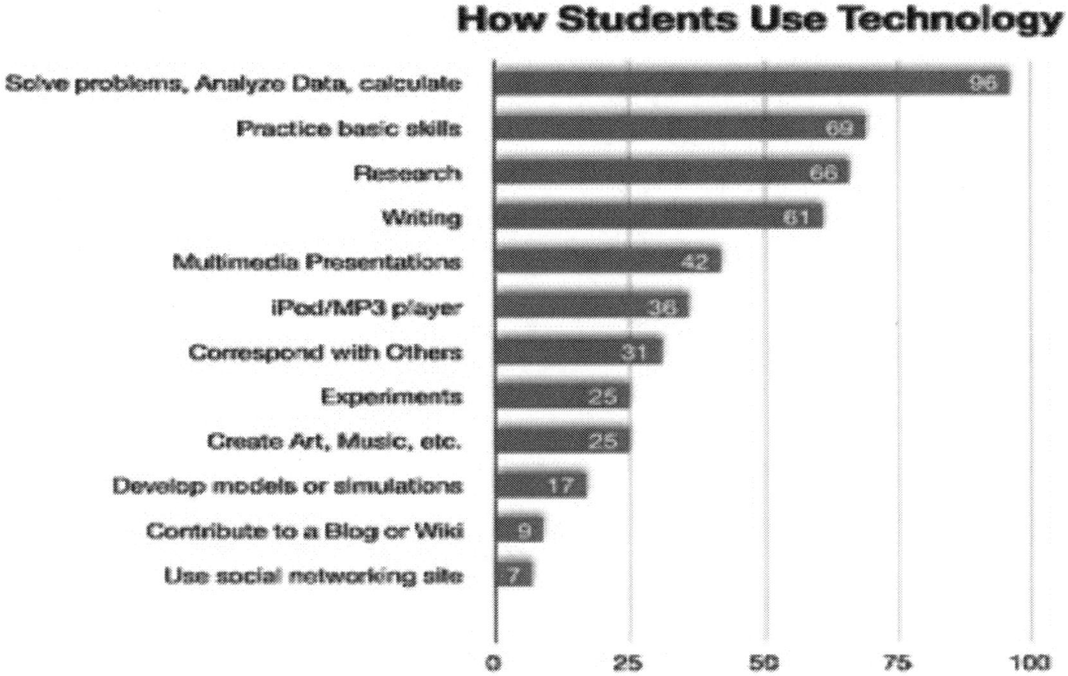

Figure 2 How students use technology (gray, et al., 2010)

While the statistics imply that quite a bit of technology is being used in classrooms, I'm skeptical. My experience as a teacher educator for the past two decades leads me to believe otherwise. For instance, the data is not clear on what teachers mean by "often" or how these tools are truly being used. I spend quite a bit of time in schools observing student teachers and walking the halls. As I peer in classroom doors, rarely do I see students using the Internet in classes in meaningful ways.

However, interactive whiteboards/smart-boards may be one recent technology changing teachers' use of the Internet in the classroom. These are devices that create a touch screen on the wall for a computer, making Internet access easy. Many districts are investing in interactive whiteboards for classrooms. Sales increased by 43% in 2009 for Smart Technologies, the leader in the field, to $648 million (Moritz, 2010) in a market of $1 billion. There are a number of studies that find that teachers using interactive whiteboards can increase student achievement (Lopez, 2010; Marzano, 2009; Schmid, 2008; Swan, Schenker, & Kratcoski, 2007) so schools are jumping on the bandwagon. However, the technology encourages teacher-directed instruction so that student-to-student interaction decreases in classrooms (Latane, 2002), the boards are very costly (approximately $4,000), and some believe that the studies indicating increased achievement are weak and funded by the industry (McCrummen, 2010).

In summary, at the end of the Internet decade, teacher use of the Internet for instruction in the classroom has not changed teaching dramatically since Cuban's research (2003) found that "the integration of computers into classroom curricula and instruction techniques was minimal." The statistics on teacher use are deceptive. While preparation for instruction and testing is certainly dominated by the Internet, teachers are not yet using the resources of the Internet for teaching students in significant ways. Interactive whiteboards are making direct instruction with the Internet more frequent in classrooms in recent years. However, multiple barriers continue to stand in the way of teachers seamlessly and meaningfully integrating the Internet into their instruction.

References

Cohen, A. & Orne, P. (2010). Report: Online Professional Development Improves Teaching and Student Achievement. Education Development Center. Retrieved from: http://www.edc.org/newsroom/press_releases/study_finds_online_professional_development_improves_teaching

Cuban, L. (1986). Teachers and Machines: The Classroom Use of Technology. New York: Teachers College Press.

Cuban, L. (2003). Oversold and Underused: Computers in the Classroom. Cambridge, MA: Harvard University Press.

DiNucci, D. (1999). Fragmented future. Print, 53(4).

Gray, L., Thomas, N., Lewis, L., Tice, P. (2010). Teachers' Use of Educational Technology in U.S. Public Schools: 2009. National Center for Education Statistics, Institute of Education Sciences, U.S. Department of Education. Washington, DC. Retrieved from http://nces.ed.gov/pubs2010/2010040.pdf.

Jenson, J., & Rose, C. (2008). Finding space for technology: Pedagogical observations on the organization of computers in school environments. Canadian Journal Of Learning And Technology, 32(1). Retrieved December 22, 2010, from http://www.cjlt.ca/index.php/cjlt/article/view/59/56

Kim, S. H., & Bagaka, J. (2005). The digital divide in students' usage of technology tools: a multilevel analysis of the role of teacher practices and classroom characteristics. Contemporary Issues in Technology and Teacher Education [Online serial], 5(3/4). Available: http://www.citejournal.org/vol5/iss3/currentpractice/article1.cfm

Kozma, R., & Schank, P. (1998). Connecting with the twenty-fist century: Technology in support of educational reform. In C. Dede (Ed.), Technology and Learning. Washington, DC; American Society for Curriculum Development.

Latane, B. (2002). Focused interactive learning: A tool for active class discussion. Teaching of Psychology, 28(1), 10-16.

Lopez, O. (2010). The Digital Learning Classroom: Improving English Language Learners' academic success in mathematics and reading using interactive whiteboard technology. Computers & Education, 54(4), 901-915.

Marzano, R. (2009). Teaching with Interactive Whiteboards, Educational Leadership, 67(3), 80–82.

McCrummen, S. (June 11, 2010). Some educators question if whiteboards, other high-tech tools raise achievement. Washington Post.

Moritz, S. (2010). Smart Technologies: Chairing the SMARTBoard market. TheStreet. Retrieved from: http://finance.yahoo.com/news/Smart-Technologies-Chairing-tsmf-3933183653.html?x=0&.v=2.

Nagel, D. (2010). Report: Mobile and Classroom Technologies Surge in Schools. theJournal. Retrieved from: http://thejournal.com/articles/2010/05/05/report-mobile-and-classroom-technologies-surge-in-schools.aspx.

National Center for Education Statistics (2000). Teachers' Tools for the 21st Century: A Report on Teachers' Use of Technology. Institute of Educational Sciences. Retrieved from: http://nces.ed.gov/surveys/frss/publications/2000102/.

Oppenheimer, T. (2004). The Flickering Mind: Saving Education from the False Promise of Technology. Random House.

Schmid, E. C. (2008). Potential pedagogical benefits and drawbacks of multimedia use in the English language classroom equipped with interactive whiteboard technology. Computers & Education, 51, 1553-1568.

Swan, K., Schenker, Kratcoski, A. (2008). The effect of the use of intereactive whiteboards on student achievement. In J. Luca & E. Weippl (Eds.), Proceedings of the World Conference on Educational Multimedia, Hypermedia, and Telecommunications 2008, 3290-3297.

Two Tin Cans and a String

Elizabeth Drake-Boyt, PhD

Professor of English, Pacific University

If the fundamental agreement between students and their instructor in carrying on a public discourse through an online class is compared to two tin cans and a string between them, what happens when one of the two ends of the string doesn't stay connected? If either the instructor or the student fails to respond across the Internet in a timely manner, then the structure of continuity and cumulative dialogue-building so crucial to the nuances of a liberal arts class falter. While the failure of an individual student to respond does not destroy the class (I call such students "flat-liners") the failure of the online instructor to respond quickly and efficiently certainly can.

At the beginning of every semester I conduct a survey in all my online classes to determine the extent of previous experiences my students have had with this kind of learning format. In order to encourage prompt responses, I attach a small extra credit point incentive. The survey helps me determine how many—and specifically who—brings online class experiences with them to my class. And it also helps me understand what those experiences have been like for them, so that I continually update my methods, materials, themes, and assignments accordingly.

Each student is invited to briefly explain his or her ideas in a discussion forum designed to be as inviting as possible. Titled "Meet and Greet," the forum is open for each student to make an introductory post and to respond to posts made by others ("You're a nurse? I'm a nurse too. . ."). This not only allows me to cheerfully encourage the timid, ease the worrier, and answer specific questions about how my class will be handled, but supplies a comparable interaction students would have in an onsite class. I "listen in" as they get acquainted, an important step toward easing an initial sense of isolation and separation. After all, taking an online class is daunting, especially if this is the student's first attempt.

In the process of monitoring threads in this introductory forum, I also gather a general idea of the initial tone of the class, assess degrees of expertise in online class taking, and identify students in terms of how they are likely to react to varying tasks: who may take a leadership role in a group presentation project, for example, who is apt to reassure fellow classmates, or who is apt to be disturbed or challenged by controversial areas, and how comfortable each is with the written format crucial to this kind of study.

Many let me know they have never taken an online class before. Others have done some learning through a hybrid class in which lecture is onsite while assignments are accomplished through Blackboard. About half to two thirds of each of my classes are fairly experienced taking classes online. In particular, I find that experienced online class takers are quite frank about what it is they don't like about online classes, and I encourage them through the "Meet and Greet" forum to clarify why.

By far the most common complaint I've heard online students express has been about an instructor's lack of communication and clarity; both for the class as a whole and for the individual student asking for greater details. Students explain the trouble with statements such as: "The teacher I had didn't answer my questions." "I did the assignments, but I never knew if I did them right or not." "The instructor didn't respond." "I didn't get much out of the class because I was confused about the deadlines." In other words, the instructor may have been holding the tin can, but somehow let the string drop.

By and large, students indicated that poor online instructors simply didn't seem to care enough to keep the class going. My question is: why would an instructor teach any class he or she is unwilling or unable to maintain—online or onsite? There might be several answers. A few years ago, I questioned an adjunct professor hired to teach a couple of online English classes through Maryland University. This was no fly-by-night, get-your-degree-quick outfit by any means, but this professor treated it as if it were. He clearly wasn't happy taking the job in the first place, and made it clear to me he was only doing it to enhance his meager income. It was also clear he felt that teaching online classes was demeaning; that it wasn't "real" teaching but more a matter of mechanically going through the motions in a way that served only the craft and not the art of teaching. Even though the University of Maryland is an accredited academic institution in good standing; his involvement with it was less desirable than if he had been hired to teach the same class onsite. His approach was to do as little as possible to "just run the class" until something better came along. I felt sorry for his students. . .

It is true that the prestige of teaching an online class is minimal if the professor desires to "step up" from teaching masses of undergraduate students their required courses into mentoring graduate students in resonating research fields. On the other hand, there are many different kinds of professors, some of whom don't worry about that angle and are simply willing and able to teach anyone—freshmen, grandmothers, ESL students, and assorted others, traditional or non-traditional, degree-seeking or not. [1]

---

[1] I have had at least four babies born to online students while taking my class, and one student's pet parrot "took" the course with him, commenting on the images viewed through lectures with

Another possible issue with teaching online classes is the perception that the authority of expertise in an academic field held by the professor is undermined. It is true that onsite classes permit the instructor more leeway to improvise in the moment; online lectures must be clearly focused on topic with little room for digressions or meanderings. [2] However, a professor secure in his or her expertise and academic standing would not find this a threatening condition. If the point is to support students in self-directed study, to mentor, foster, facilitate, or otherwise share an interest in the course material, then this can be accomplished as well online as onsite. So a good online instructor is one accepting of the forum in the first place, and one dedicated foremost to serve the diversity of students in the class.

Certainly, placing an instructor in a class assumes a desire to teach it, just as placing a student in a class assumes a willingness to put forward the effort to successfully complete it. Everyone has different talents and strengths, and this is especially true in the academic professions. The strength of an institution of learning depends upon the ability of its administration to fit instructors to classes the way Mozart likened an aria "to fit a singer like a well-cut suit of clothes." Just as it would be foolish to ask an elementary school teacher to teach graduate university students, so it would be foolish to ask a professor who has a low opinion of online classes to teach them.

---

favor or disfavor. This kind of interaction with students binds them with the instructor under the common denominator of being human beings above all other diverse conditions.

[2] Discussion boards and individual emails do permit digressions; however, it is the option of students to read or ignore them, as may be appropriate. In an onsite class, everyone is "captive" to the digression, and a common complaint of onsite students is that the professor "rambles".

Two Tin Cans and a String: Teaching Liberal Arts Online

Elizabeth Drake-Boyt, PhD

Professor of English, Pacific University

#1 Toolbox Basics

Remember that old-time kids' "telephone" entertainment of stretching a string taut between two tin cans? Magically, voices sounded as if they were right next to each other despite the fact that the speakers were not visible to one another. There were a few limitations. For example, it was important to take turns; one person spoke while the other listened in a cumulative sequence of conversation or it didn't work. And sooner or later, someone forgot to keep the string tight so the flow of conversation was interrupted. It was very simple; a tool that got the job done. Two tin cans and a string served the basic arrangement of all public discourse; listening and speaking in turn to build a cumulative exchange of information, shape ideas, formulate plans, or manage negotiations.

These communicative needs are still met if both parties are physically near enough to one another to hear each other's voices, as would be the case for an onsite liberal arts classroom at a university. However, the requirement of having everyone involved in the discourse physically present isn't always possible. For that, we needed tools with which to enhance our voices.

Enter the radically new and mysterious invention of writing and reading. First, clay tablets (rather bulky and prone to breakage) and later paper (scrolls to books) bore the marks of one person at a distance of time and/or space to represent the spoken voice. And most wonderful, these written symbols seen by a reader could be reconverted from symbolic markings into spoken language again for all present to hear at any time and in the same way; the written marks endured time and so were permanent records. The skills of reading and writing were highly prized public property. Until books could be printed in quantity, it was considered very rude of a reader to keep a piece of writing—even a personal letter—to himself in the presence of others. [1]

Writing has become one of those essential tools of communication to be used or misused according to the skills or purposes of the writer. And it has revolutionized all social, political and economic intra- and intercultural

[1] When I conveyed letters from a student in the United States to his wife in Katmandu, Nepal in the early spring of 1971, the entire extended family of twenty-five gathered together and listened intently as the wife read them aloud.

exchanges, including education. So we take it for granted that in any given classroom there are many teachers—one physically present, while others teach through their writings in textbooks used in the class.
Later, the radical and mysterious technologies of photography, cinema, and television were added to the public discourse toolbox. These media placed human representations of communication across asynchronous time and distance that were accepted as "real" in very much the same way as synchronous encounters. When, around 1895, the Méliès brothers first projected the moving image of a train approaching on the white wall of a Paris café, patrons fled in terror. How often have we spoken of sitcom characters as if they were real people we've met face to face, or described the televised documentation of a news event as if we'd experienced it first-hand? Regardless of the medium, the visceral connection between an immediate physical presence and its symbolic representation still haunts our collective psyche. From "phone sex" to radios anthropomorphically designed to evoke the features of a human face, we "connect" to this kind of virtual experience as if it was an equitable exchange.

Now we have the equally radical and mysterious communication tool of the Internet. As with all new tools, one of the first things people manage to do with it is figure out how to make some money from it. There are beneficial uses and detrimentally destructive abuses of the new medium. But while the physical object of a book makes it easier to copyright its contents, regulate and market, the Internet bears some of the ephemeral immediacy of face to face conversation. As Issac Gilman effectively pointed out in his December 2010 Interface article titled, "Open Opportunities: The Impact of the Internet on Academic Libraries", most people using the Internet from the beginning believe it should be free and available to all as a fundamental human right, just as if it was another form of face to face conversation. [2]

The tool of the Internet is facile, mutable and immediate. Out of the basic capacity of email (which some of us "old fogies" accustomed to writing letters and sending them through the US Postal Service loyally stick to despite a galaxy of other online formats) the same basic purpose is served at the speed of light. It still requires two or more people taking turns speaking and reading/ listening through a cumulative discourse. And more than that; the Internet not only places communicants in a two-way exchange, but also in a synchronous web of possible other relevant exchanges, all at the speed of light.

Oddly enough, this mode of communication is not all that different from the setup of a liberal arts classroom; teachers, students, and relevant written

---

[2] Gillman, Issac. 2010. "Open Opportunities: The Impact of the Internet on Academic Libraries." Interface, Vol. 10, Issue 10, December 2010. Accessed December 21, 2010. http://bcis.pacificu.edu/journal/article.php?id=748

material available with which to not only exchange information, but (as is so dear to liberal arts curriculums) frame the methodologies of critical thinking in a public forum. Someone speaks, and there follows a cascade of relevant considerations based on that communication. A wonderful set of tools skillfully and effectively employed produces the satisfaction and investment in learning. The Internet is no different in that regard; it's just another set of tools we can learn to use, and bring its benefits (while respecting its limitations) into the service of education.

Gaming – Volume 11

Jamaica King – *Is Runeterra a Website, or Is It a Real Community*
http://bcis.pacificu.edu/interface/?p=416

Christopher J. Ferguson – *'m Games Are Like Smoking and Lung Cancer' and Other Urban Legends in the Violent Video Game Debate*
http://bcis.pacificu.edu/interface/?p=221

Is Runeterra a Website, or Is It a Real Community?

Jamaica King
Berglund Student Fellow, Pacific University

Definitions

A community is "a social, religious, occupational, or other group sharing common characteristics or interests and perceived or perceiving itself as distinct in some respect from the larger society within which it exists".[1] In short, a community is a group, brought together by shared interests or common ideology. In social psychology, group is defined as "a collection of people who are perceived to be bonded together in a coherent unit to some degree".[2] This analysis is a case study focusing on the League of Legends fan-site entitled Runeterra. The purpose of this article is to identify the elements that define Runeterra as a community and briefly examine the benefits of joining a group, with examples from this specific website.

Runeterra

In April 2010, Brandon "Roku" Davis officially launched Runeterra, a small online gaming community that focuses on League of Legends, a multiplayer online battle arena (MOBA) game developed by Riot Games. It is intended to provide its members with insightful League of Legends analysis and discussions. Runeterra is home to about 200 active users, serving as an online medium for meaningful communication and interaction among its community members. Runeterrans originate from various locations throughout the globe, brought together via the Internet. Since Runeterra is a virtual community, it relies solely on the availability of the Internet, and without internet access, a member is either temporarily disengaged or permanently disassociated.

---

[1] http://dictionary.reference.com/browse/community
[2] Baron, R. A., Branscombe, N. R., & Byrne, D. (2008). Social Psychology. Allyn & Bacon, p. 380.

Types of Groups

There are 2 different types of groups, which differ in the way its members are bonded. The first type is labeled *common-identity group* and is defined as a group whose members are linked together via a category as a whole.[3] Examples of common-identity groups include groups that are categorized by nationality (e.g., Canadian), ethnicity (e.g., Korean), or location of schools (e.g., Pacific University students). The second type is called *common-bond groups*, in which individual members are bonded to each other. Examples of common bond groups include teams (e.g., Counter Logic Gaming, SoloMid) work teams (e.g., Runeterra writers), or larger communities such as clgaming.net and solomid.net.
Groups differ in entitativity, the extent to which they are perceived as coherent entities. [4] The characteristics of groups high in entitativity are:

1. members interact with one another often
2. the group is of consequence to its members
3. members share common goals and
4. they are similar to one another in important ways.[5]

Runeterra is moderately high in entitativity. Members are constantly interacting via multiple means for communication (e.g., forum [6], live-chat [7], Twitter [8], Steam [9]). The Runeterra community is important to its members because individuals actually make the effort to participate (e.g., communication, contests) and advocate for the group or group members (e.g., watching members' live stream, aid in live stream advertisement). Runeterrans share a common goal: interest in League of Legends. They are also similar to one another such that they possess an interest in the game and value insightful knowledge and discussion.

[3] Ibid
[4] Ibid
[5] Ibid
[6] http://runeterra.com/formus/index.php
[7] http://runeterra.com/irc.php
[8] http://twitter.com/#!/Runeterra
[9] http://steamcommunity.com/groups/runeterra

Key Components of Group

There are four key components that exist in essentially every group: (1) status, (2) roles, (3) norms, and (4) cohesiveness. [10]

- Status

In many groups, members vary in status, individuals' position or rank within the group. [11] Within the Runeterra community, members have a level associated with their account. Level is positively correlated with communication activity. Specifically, on the forums when a member reaches a certain number of posts, he or she gains a level. This is an explicit example of status. An implicit example of rank is seniority–how long a member is involved or a part of the community. This is based on the date a member joined the community (i.e., account creation). This metric is somewhat flawed in that it does not account for long time lurkers, who register at a later date.

Status is interdependent with roles. In some cases, people with high rank roles possess higher status. In Runeterra, administrators, writers, and moderators bear higher status because they earned it through their roles. They also stand out from the general audience through their roles.

- Roles

Roles are a set of behaviors associated with a specific position that individuals within a group are expected to perform.[12] In some cases, roles are assigned, but at other times, they may be acquired formally or informally. Runeterran writers and streamers generally acquire their roles by contacting Roku or through recruitment (e.g., another writer recruits them, members refer writers). Roles aid to provide members an opportunity to foster a sense of relatedness. When members develop this feeling of belonging, chances of member retention increase.

- Norms

Every group has a set of norms, which are rules or expectations within a group about how its members should or should not behave.[13] Runeterra too has these

---

[10] Baron, R. A., Branscombe, N. R., & Byrne, D. (2008). Social Psychology. Allyn & Bacon, p. 382.
[11] Ibid, p. 383
[12] Ibid, p. 384
[13] Ibid, p. 387

norms. They are not explicitly introduced in the forums, but community members abide by these rules. Some of Runeterra's implicit norms include:

- No trolling [14]
- No pointless posting
- Respect

These are examples of some norms shared within this particular community, but it is not limited to these expectations.

- Cohesion

The last element of group is cohesiveness, the quality that compel group members to remain in the group.[15] A crucial aspect of cohesive groups is solidarity; that is, group members see themselves as homogenous, cooperative with one another, supportive of each other, and work together to achieve the group goals. Runeterrans are homogenous to a degree in that they are all interested in League of Legends. They cooperate with one another to play inhouses [16] and also support each other (e.g., watching other members' stream, commenting on members' forum posts). The goal of the website community is to provide insightful League of Legends analysis and discussion. Group members collaborate to achieve this goal by giving constructive criticism and contributing new knowledge.

According to the Social Brain Hypothesis, as the size of a group increases, cohesiveness decreases.[17] Since Runeterra is a fairly small community, it is moderately more cohesive than larger communities such as clgaming.net or the forum community on the official League of Legends site. But when the community expands, cohesiveness may slowly decrease.

Cohesiveness may also decrease as a result of a schism - splintering of a group into multiple other groups due to a change in ideology and disagreement among members. [18] For example if Runeterra's goals changed, members who disagree or those who are no longer interested in the new goals for the group will eventually leave the community.

---

[14] http://www.urbandictionary.com/define.php?term=trolling

[15] Baron, R. A., Branscombe, N. R., & Byrne, D. (2008). Social Psychology. Allyn & Bacon, p. 388.

[16] http://www.urbandictionary.com/define.php?term=inhouse

[17] Dunbar, R. (1998). The social brain hypothesis. Evolutionary Anthropology, pp. 178 – 190.

[18] Baron, R. A., Branscombe, N. R., & Byrne, D. (2008). Social Psychology. Allyn & Bacon, p. 392.

Benefits of Joining a Group

People are attracted to a myriad of groups for various reasons. One rationale for why individuals seek to belong to groups is to gain self-knowledge. [19] Group membership is vital to our self-concept; we learn what kind of person we are and want to be. Through my experiences as a member of Runeterra, I came to realize that I am passionate about making people happy. I developed an interest in hosting and planning contests as a way to make League of Legend fans happier.

Another benefit of joining a group is the ability for members to help each other achieve both group and individual goals. Within groups, individuals can seek self-enhancement or self-transcendence. Self-enhancement is the boosting of one's public image. [20] Runeterra allows for its members to engage in self-enhancement through writing, streaming, and contest creation. Members of its community are able to build a resume or increase status and public image through roles. Runeterra also offers its members self-transcendence, realized through helping others. [21] Runeterrans are constantly interacting in the forums or live-chat to help each other improve (e.g., gameplay, knowledge) or simply provide constructive criticism or opinion.

---

[19] Tajfel, H., & Turner, J. C. (1986). The social identity theory of intergroup behavior. In S. Worchel & W. G. Austin (Eds.), The social psychology of intergroup relations (2nd ed., pp. 7-24). Monterrey, CA: Brooks-Cole.
[20] Baron, R. A., Branscombe, N. R., & Byrne, D. (2008). Social Psychology. Allyn & Bacon, p. 390.
[21] Ibid

Conclusion

Runeterra is a website, but it is also an online gaming community, with members who coalesce for insightful League of Legends analysis and discussion. It is a common-bond group that is bonded by League of Legends and the desire for more astute knowledge. The community is moderately high in entitativity and contains the four key components of a group. The benefits of joining Runeterra includes gaining self-knowledge, self-enhancement, and self-transcendence. But most importantly, like most communities, Runeterra administrators and moderators must continually assesses the demands of the community, create a model for change, implement the plans, and evolve accordingly.

'Video Games Are Like Smoking and Lung Cancer' and Other Urban Legends in the Violent Video Game Debate

Christopher J. Ferguson
Assistant Professor, Texas A&M International University

According to the Merriam-Webster dictionary, an urban legend is "An often lurid story or anecdote that is based on hearsay and often reported as true" (Merriam-Webster, 2010). Most typically the term is applied to stories of vanishing hitchhikers, hook-bearing murderers and such; they are tales of uncertain origin, told as if true, and tend to carry a moral message for society (Croft, 2006). In conducting research on video game violence and watching the debates among politicians, pressure groups and scholars in this realm, I have observed the repetition of several claims or stories by all three groups. Stories which are often (although not always as we'll see) of uncertain origin, are told as if true (but in each case are demonstrably false) and contain a moral message designed to encourage others to act on an issue the storyteller views as pressing.

I adapt the concept of an urban legend to include these scientific urban legends. Like contemporary urban legends, scientific urban legends can be identified by the following hall-marks:

- 1.) They are stated as absolute fact. In the case of a scientific urban legend the statement at hand has either been debunked in the published literature, or at the very least, is highly controversial. Despite this, the statement is still communicated as absolute fact, without any mention of the debunking literature or controversy. The notion that violent video games have caused an ((non-existent)) epidemic of school shootings or youth violence is are an example.

- 2.) The basis of the story remains unclear. The claim that there are 3,500 studies of media violence with only 18 not finding harmful effects is one such example. This statement was repeated by no less than the American Academy of Pediatrics (Cook, 2000) despite the fact that no one has any idea where these figures came from, only that they are demonstrably untrue (Freedman, 2002). Sometimes a claim can be traced back to a single source (e.g. Bushman & Anderson, 2001; Grossman, 1996), although the origins of the claim remained mired in unclear logic or questionable statistics.

- 3.) The messages are the most frightening possible...making wild claims of scientific certainty regarding inevitable and serious harm. Nonsense claims that media violence may explain upwards of 30% of societal violence (Strasburger, 2007) would fit in this category, as would long-debunked claims, equating the effect size of media violence research to hard science demonstrations, such as the relationship between smoking and lung cancer.

The issue of video game violence has attracted a great deal of societal attention. It is now well understood historically that new media tend to provoke patterns of moral panic in which such urban legends are common (Ferguson, 2010; Kutner & Olson, 2008). For instance in the 19th century, experts claimed young women should not read dDime nNovels due to the alleged inability of women to distinguish reality from fiction. Similarly, in the 1950s,, psychiatric experts testified before the U.S. Senate that the characters Batman and Robin, in comic books, were secretly a gay couple who would lead children to delinquency and homosexuality. It is an unfortunate aspect of all such media in moral panics that not only politicians and pressure groups, but also scholars can be counted on to make extreme claims that violate the traditions of scientific conservatism, skepticism and careful observation.

Perhaps the first of the video game urban legends was the belief that violent games were "linked" with school shooting incidents. This was a common refrain following the 1999 Columbine High Massacre, regularly indulged in by politicians and pressure groups. Unfortunately, some scholars also joined in this litany, making claims that many school shootings were "linked" to violent games (e.g. Anderson, 2004). Of course almost all young men play violent games at least occasionally, so making such "links" are not difficult. Despite the fact that older adults commit as many, if not more, mass shootings as do teenagers, it's interesting to observe that the issue of violent games never arises when an older adult commits mass homicide (tenure was the boogeyman in the recent case of a female biology professor in Alabama). The supposed video game link was laid to rest in 2002 by the U.S. Secret Service which found no evidence for such a link. Yet it continues to be resurrected.

Arguably, more pernicious is the argument that the effects of video game violence on aggression are similar to those for smoking and lung cancer or similar medical effects (Bushman & Anderson, 2001). Such a wild claim should have attracted great scrutiny, but instead has been uncritically repeated by politicians and some scholars. Unlike the school shooting claim, the 3,500 studies claim, and the interactivity claim discussed later, the lung cancer urban legend is clearly attributed to Bushman and Anderson (2001) who used some dubious statistics to make this claim. These statistics have since been debunked in the published literature (Block & Crain, 2007; Ferguson, 2009). Nonetheless politicians and some scholars continue to repeat this claim without making any mention of the debunking articles. Of course any comparison between the dubious outcome measures used in most aggression studies and the unquestionable validity of deaths from smoking is fraught with error. But even taken at face value, the two bodies of research and the research results they produce aren't remotely similar.

Another common urban legend is that the U.S. military uses video games to desensitize soldiers so that they will kill more reliably. The origins of this particular idea seems to lay with David Grossman (1996), although he refers to some earlier U.S. Army work, comparing the rates at which U.S. soldiers in World War II fired at the enemy with those of modern U.S. infantrymen, such as during the first Gulf War. Results indicating that the conscripted, often rudimentarily trained farmers, schoolteachers and lawyers, called to duty during World War II, were handed a semi-automatic M1 and told to fire at identifiable targets, shot less often than the highly trained volunteer career infantrymen, firing fully automatic M-16s, while using night-vision goggles and were instructed to fire in the general direction of the enemy.

Despoite all the differences between the two groups, Grossman focused on the advent of simulations in training as the crucial difference; hence an urban legend was born. Never mind that the U.S. Army has denied these claims (video games are used for vehicle and team training and decision making and even recruitment, but not desensitization) or that police organizations use similar simulations to reduce impulsive "bad" shootings. Nor does it seem to matter that today's youth, consuming far greater amounts of violent games than any past generation possibly could, are the least violent youth in 40 years. The sound byte is repeated often, presumably given itsbecause of its emotional appeal.

Lastly, I address the claim that the interactivity of video games makes them more harmful than other media. This argument was one basis for California's recent anti-game law. However, though it is often repeated as speculation, by now the evidence is clear that, even taken at face value, media violence research finds no evidence for an increased effect for video games (Ferguson & Kilburn, 2009; Sherry, 2001). Politicians and even some scholars, nonetheless, repeat this claim ad infinitum, despite that it is long past time to lay it to rest. One gets the sense that the motivation for repeating this belief is that it must be true according to those that proposed the theory. Unfortunately the research evidence has not lined up to support it.

One expects the repetition of urban legends by pressure/activists groups with a clear axe to grind. What is more disappointing is how often some scholars have indulged in repeating these urban legends uncritically. Of course it is now known that pressure/activist groups such as the National Institute of Media and the Family or the Center for Successful Parenting have funded much of the "anti-game" literature. As such, I argue that the line between the advocacy of these pressure groups and the science funded by these groups may have been hopelessly blurred. When scientists step into the public eye and repeat nonsense urban legends...whether that Batman and Robin were gay or that video game research can be compared to smoking/lung cancer research, scholars cause a great embarrassment to the scientific enterprise. Once society begins to realize that the extreme claims made are not coming true, and I argue this is beginning to happen for video game research, the damage done to science can be very significant. Therefore, I call upon scholars on all sides of this debate to exert far greater conservatism in the claims being made, and to remain alert for the potential that they themselves may be repeating, or even creating, scientific urban legends.

References

Anderson, C. (2004). An update on the effects of playing violent video games. Journal of Adolescence, 27, 113-122.

Block, J., & Crain, B. (2007). Omissions and errors in 'Media violence and the American public.' American Psychologist, 62, 252-253.

Bushman, B., & Anderson, C. (2001). Media violence and the American public. American Psychologist, 56, 477-489.

Cook, D. (2000). Testimony of the American Academy of Pediatrics on media violence before the U.S. Senate Commerce Committee. Elk Grove Village, IL: American Academy of Pediatrics. Available at: http://www.aap.org/advocacy/releases/mediaviolencetestimony.pdf.

Croft, R. (2006). Folklore, families and fear: Exploring the influence of the oral tradition on consumer decision-making. Journal of Marketing Management, 22, 1053-1076.

Ferguson, C. J. (2010). Blazing Angels or Resident Evil? Can violent video games be a force for good? Review of General Psychology, 14(2) 68-81.

Ferguson. C. J., & Kilburn, J. (2009). The Public health risks of media violence: A meta-analytic review. Journal of Pediatrics,154(5), 759-763.

Ferguson, C. J. (2009). Is psychological research really as good as medical research? Effect size comparisons between psychology and medicine. Review of General Psychology, 13(2), 130-136.

Freedman, J. (2002). Media violence and its effect on aggression.: Assessing the scientific evidence. Toronto: University of Toronto Press.

Grossman, D. (1996). On killing: The psychological cost of learning to kill in war and society. Boston: Back Bay Books.

Kutner, L., & Olson, C. (2008). Grand theft childhood: The surprising truth about violent video games and what parents can do. New York: Simon & Schuster.

Merrian-Webster Dictionary. (2010). Retrieved 12/3/10 from: http://www.merriam-webster.com/dictionary/urban%20legend.

Sherry, J. (2001). The effects of violent video games on aggression: A meta-analysis. Human Communication Research, 27, 409-431.

Strasburger, V. (2007). Go ahead punk, make my day: It's time for pediatricians to take action against media violence. Pediatrics, 119, e1398-1399.

Media – Volume 11

Nicole Nowlin – *The Digital Frontier of Manga Part I*
http://bcis.pacificu.edu/interface/?p=350

Nicole Nowlin – *The Digital Frontier of Manga Part II*
http://bcis.pacificu.edu/interface/?p=473

Jake Fischer – *The End of Sound Slavery*
http://bcis.pacificu.edu/interface/?p=270

The Digital Frontier of Manga Part I

By Nicole Nowlin, Berglund
Berglund Student Fellow, Pacific University

“I’m a believer in digital,” said Kuo-Yu Liang of Diamond Distributors in an article published by Publisher’s Weekly. “I’ve preferred reading an e-book over a ‘real’ book for over 10 years, so I’m excited about every new thing… But, it doesn’t matter what I believe. Look at what’s happening to music, movies, newspapers, magazines, and gaming. The future of reading is in the digital format, get used to it.” [1] The Japanese digital market was estimated at $654.5 million in 2009 and expected to reach $797.3 million in 2010. The 2011 estimate was even higher at $904.4 million. Growth of downloads was expected in multiple formats, with a decreasing growth trend expected, but a steady overall download rate. The industry also estimates that 89% of digital publishing in Japan is manga.[2]

In 2010, the US and Canadian comic publishing industry took a hard hit. The comic market was worth $680 million in 2009, and $370 million was in graphic novels. Japanese manga itself declined 20%, marking a third year of decline. For an industry with two prior years of sales drops, that could equal up to 50% in three years, as well as marking the downsizing or closing of several publishers. However, digital comic sales were predicted to increase nearly ten times in 2010. In 2009, the digital publishing of comics was a $500,000 industry, but the projection for 2010 put it at $6 to $8 million as “the fastest-growing part of the comics business,” according to an article by ICv2. There isn’t “anything we can do to fight it, so we have to figure out how to exploit it and expand business.”[3]

With my previous fellowship, I took the opportunity to examine the scanlation internet phenomenon, a sort of illegal version of digital comic publishing. They can be viewed in previous issues of Interface and are a useful background for this series of articles (Part 1, Part 2, Part 3)[4] [5] [6] Using this illegal digital manga

---

[1] Reid, Calvin. "DBD's Liang Finds Graphic Novel Growth Abroad." *Publishers Weekly*. 23 Nov. 2010. Web. <http://www.publishersweekly.com/pw/by-topic/industry-news/bookselling/article/45276-dbd-s-liang-finds-graphic-novel-growth-abroad.html>.

[2] Shimizu, Masaaki. Interview. *ICv2*. 27 Sept. 2010. Web. <http://www.icv2.com/articles/news/18434.html>.

[3] Hudson, Laura. "ICv2 Projects Graphic Novel Sales Down 20%, Digital Comics Up Over 1000% in 2010." *ComicsAlliance*. 7 Oct. 2010. Web. <http://www.comicsalliance.com/2010/10/07/digital-comics-sales/>.

[4] http://bcis.pacificu.edu/journal/article.php?id=633

[5] http://bcis.pacificu.edu/journal/article.php?id=729

[6] http://bcis.pacificu.edu/journal/article.php?id=737

community as a springboard, I felt the logical evolution of my fellowship project would be to look at the opposite side of the spectrum – i.e., the legal digital manga world. With that in mind, I will take a look at the evolution of e-manga, the trials facing the adoptions of this media, and the future of the manga industry on the digital frontier.

To recap, scanlations are illegally scanned and translated (hence "scan+lations") Japanese manga. As the previous articles stated, it is not simply something that was traded among friends or circles, and moderately difficult to find. It was easily accessible online and still is, despite the threatened legal action and an organized publishers' coalition. At the San Diego Comic Con in 2010, a panel of industry experts spoke on digital piracy and the future of online manga. [7] With the serious threat of scanlations worrying publishers and the new coalition worrying fans, such a panel was to be expected. Although not heavily attended, the topic of the future of online manga was a timely one. With applications like "All Manga Reader" [8] available as extensions to browser and automatically pulling from illegal scanlation sites, the task of capturing the online manga market is a daunting one for publishers.

Manga piracy affects companies and their partners, such as the retailers, writers, distributors, and the creators. Ed Chavez, of Vertical, Inc., a small publisher, explained in an article by ComicsAlliance that while traditional publishers enjoy lowered costs for distributing digital content, manga can be a far more expensive publishing process. The licenses are expensive normally, but licensors may require new licenses with new terms and higher royalties to allow digital publications. He says printing is only 10% of a book's costs, and that additional fees make up more than 50%. Digital royalties may go up 5 to 10%. In 2009, Japan, the home of manga, saw an over 6% drop in manga sales, and a 10% drop in manga magazine sales. [9] Piracy also affects the licensing abilities of US companies, thereby affecting the fans that do not see the titles they want, sending them to scanlation sites – essentially becoming another step in the self-sustaining cycle of piracy and publication. The scanlation aggregator sites with which publishers would need to compete earn money from advertisements, whereas publishers will need to find a way to monetize e-manga in a profitable manner.

---

[7] Aoki, Deb. "From Manga Scanlations to Comics on the IPad: Online Piracy Panel at Comic-Con." *Manga About.com*. 11 Aug. 2010. Web. <http://manga.about.com/b/2010/08/11/from-manga-scanlations-to-comics-on-the-ipad-online-piracy-panel-at-comic-con.htm>.

[8] Kleefeld, Sean. "Justifying Illegal Scanlations?" Web log post. *Kleefeld on Comics*. 17 Nov. 2010. Web. <http://kleefeldoncomics.blogspot.com/2010/11/justifying-illegal-scanlations.html>.

[9] Chavez, Ed, Michael Gombos, and Marco Pavia. "The Manga Industry Speaks: Taking Stock in Tough Times." Interview by David Brothers. *ComicsAlliance*. 20 Aug. 2010. Web. <http://www.comicsalliance.com/2010/08/20/the-manga-industry-speaks-taking-stock-in-tough-times/>.

There are numerous ways a person can read material online. E-readers have been released from numerous companies, some with more success than others. The iPad, while not predating the eReader market, was a game changer that forced greater competition for the attention of consumers. Publishers started creating apps for the iPad, essentially the first legitimate digital manga reading option. It is important to note that just as with the previously mentioned browser extension, there were apps created that accumulated illegal scanlations as well. Some groups, like Katalyst Lab, went for exclusive digital comics, as with the release of "Maniac Tours" in the App Store only. The first episode was available for free, with subsequent episodes available for $0.99 each. The publication was also released simultaneously in English, Japanese, and French.[10] Digital content is easier to produce in multiple languages and allows access to a greater number of users. For independent authors, like Mike Jasper and Niki Smith of *In Maps and Legends*, and Alex DeCampi of *Valentine*, publishing across all Apple platforms and others, such as the Barnes & Noble Nook, provides an advantage to their publications that will be integral in the developing digital market for comics.[11]

Tokyopop, perhaps the largest manga publisher in the United States, launched an iPad/iPod app for their PRIEST manga series at Comic Con in 2010.

---

[10] "IPad Manga Comic Maniac Tours Now On Sale." *Anime News Network*. 6 Nov. 2010. Web. <http://www.animenewsnetwork.com/press-release/2010-11-06/ipad-maniac-tours-on-sale>.

[11] Alverson, Brigid. "2010: The Year in Digital Comics." *Robot 6*. Comic Book Resources, 2 Jan. 2011. Web. <http://robot6.comicbookresources.com/2011/01/2010-the-year-in-digital-comics/>.

They've also begun working with digital library distributors, such as Zinio and Overdrive, and expect to provide more titles in the near future. Tokyopop is looking into additional media delivery options as well. Smaller publishers, like Vertical Inc., uses iTunes and the App Store to distribute its Tezuka series through "AstroBoy Magazine" and is also pursuing other forms of publishing, including talks with Sony to provide manga through the Sony PlayStation Network.[12] Viz Manga, another major manga publisher in the United States, was one of the first to jump on the iPad bandwagon for digital content. They created a free app that provided previews of their books at no cost, with the ability to purchase the books and keep them in the app like a virtual bookshelf.[13] The first five series offered were at $4.99 per volume, less than the cover price of the print manga. They also offered volume one of the popular Death Note manga for free as an incentive to download the app.[14] From examining the prices of e-books, I've found many are as expensive as their printed counterparts, as strange as that may seem. Viz's price appears quite reasonable in that respect.

Viz also thought ahead with regards to online reading of manga, and launched its site sigikki.com. On SIGIKKI, thirteen series from Viz's Signature line are available for free reading and review. If reader demand supports the series, then they are printed in the signature line. Web comics are done much the same way; gathering fans and then offering print copies if sufficiently popular, sometimes as a full volume like a graphic novel or only one chapter at a time like a comic book. It provides a built in risk limitation.[15] Now, if only movies could do the same thing, we wouldn't see so many millions wasted on box office flops. Crunchyroll, a site that provides streaming Japanese anime and Asian dramas, contracted with Japanese technology company, Bitly, to build a viewing platform for manga. While this spurred some fans to think Crunchyroll would be entering the digital manga business, they have created the platform for others to use, not to use for licensing titles themselves.[16]

---

[12] Chavez, Ed, Michael Gombos, and Marco Pavia. "The Manga Industry Speaks: Taking Stock in Tough Times." Interview by David Brothers. *ComicsAlliance*. 20 Aug. 2010. Web. <http://www.comicsalliance.com/2010/08/20/the-manga-industry-speaks-taking-stock-in-tough-times/>.

[13] "VIZ Manga App - Manga on Your IPad!" *VIZ Media*. Web. <http://www.viz.com/apps/>.

[14] Reid, Calvin. "Viz Media Releases Free Viz Manga App for the IPad." *Publishers Weekly*. 2 Nov. 2010. Web. <http://www.publishersweekly.com/pw/by-topic/book-news/comics/article/45034-viz-media-releases-free-viz-manga-app-for-the-ipad.html>.

[15] Brothers, David. "SIGIKKI.com: Alt-Manga and Digital Comics from Viz - ComicsAlliance | Comics Culture, News, Humor, Commentary, and Reviews." *ComicsAlliance*. 9 Mar. 2010. Web. <http://www.comicsalliance.com/2010/03/09/sigikki-com-alt-manga-and-digital-comics-from-viz/>.

[16] Aoki, Deb. "Kun Gao, CEO of Crunchyroll Interview – Q & A with Kun Gao About Crunchyroll's Online Manga Publishing Platform." *Manga About.com*. Summer 2010. Web. <http://manga.about.com/od/mangaeditorsinterviews/a/Interview-Kun-Gao-Of-Crunchyroll.htm>.

Not all publishers are coming out with formats that are particularly sensitive to their end users. Yen Press is following a similar scheme for online publishing in a serialized format, with a digital relaunch of their publication *Yen Plus*. It is a preview of their print manga being offered in a paid format digitally for $2.99 a month.[17] This doesn't sound as appealing or interesting to a reader, seeing as how it is previews only – there would be no completed content or continuing chapters for a reader to look forward to. A reader could just as easily hit the bookstore and read the back cover or flip through the first few pages without paying the monthly fee.

Another potential flop in the digital publishing domain would be Square Enix's opening of its own manga store online. While Square Enix is known among gamers for famous works, such as the *Final Fantasy* series, and for working with Disney on *Kingdom Hearts*, they are not well known as a manga publisher. Their most well known titles are actually licensed and distributed in English by the aforementioned US publisher Viz. Like Viz, the online price is lower than the print price of a new book ($5.99) but is suggested to be "for a limited time" and therefore may be expected to rise. It is also not downloadable. While Apple Apps, like the Viz app, are not downloadable in the sense that you can access every file you purchase independently without the reader, they do not require the internet to be connected to read what has been purchased. Square Enix will be using a browser reader that will require a person to be online at the time to read their purchase – not exactly convenient for someone on the go looking for a digital copy of their favorite title.[18]

---

[17] Cha, Kai-Ming. "After Scanlations: Manga Publishers Look to Offer Legal Digital Access." *Publishers Weekly*. 24 Aug. 2010. Web. <http://www.publishersweekly.com/pw/by-topic/book-news/comics/article/44242-after-scanlations-manga-publishers-look-to-offer-legal-digital-access.html>.

[18] "Square Enix Launches Manga Store: Some Concerns." Best Deal Media, 31 Dec. 2010. Web. <http://www.bestdealmedia.info/2839/square-enix-launches-manga-store-some-concerns.html>.

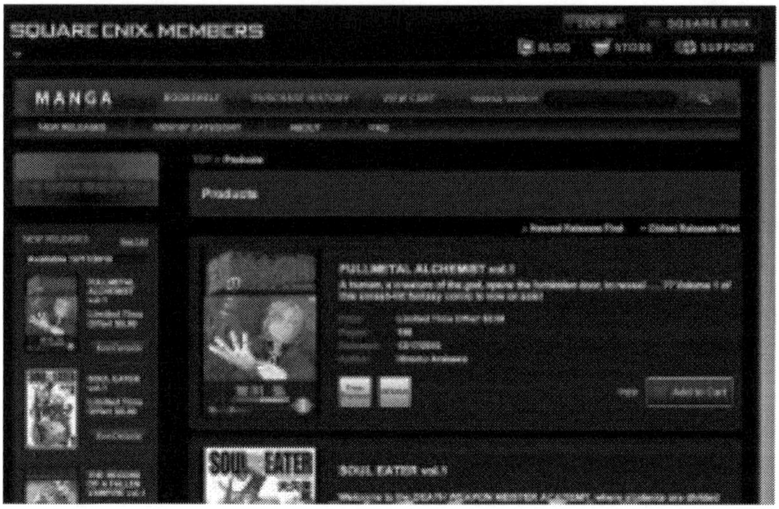

One former scanlation site, Mangahelpers.com, is looking to legitimize itself through the creation of Open Manga. While the platform was announced last June, and the group was in contact with Japanese publishers, there have been no updates from the new site's blog in several months, suggesting the program may have failed before it truly began.[19] [20] Toshiba attempted to enter the world of digital publishing through a site called Manganovel. Its purpose was to digitally distribute various types of manga over the internet and to not be restricted to one publisher such as Viz. It was more like the new J Manga Portal that is in the works mentioned later in this article. Manganovel died a quiet death, for reasons unknown.[21] Perhaps it entered the digital manga frontier too early, as it was before scanlations had been targeted for legal action.

A new up-and-coming digital manga site is similar to Manganovel and of special note. The Digital Manga Guild, the brainchild of Digital Manga, Inc., President Hikaru Sasahara, is slated to take the online manga publishing industry by storm with perfect timing.

19 *Open Manga - Coming Soon!* Web. <http://openmanga.org/index.php>.
20 Nimloth. Web log post. *MangaHelpers*. 11 June 2010. Web. <http://mangahelpers.com/news/details/377>.
21 "Toshiba, Manganovel Offer User-Translated Manga Online." *Anime News Network*. 1 Oct. 2007. Web. <http://www.animenewsnetwork.com/news/2007-10-01/toshiba-manganovel-offer-user-translated-manga-online>.

At Yaoi Con 2010, President Sasahara announced the new program that would take the recently targeted scanlators and hire them to perform legal translations of manga for digital distribution. With Digital Manga, Inc., acting as the go-between, between publishers in Japan and pre-screened scanlating groups online. The three players would produce manga in English for distribution online through the Digital Manga, Inc., eManga platform. Popular titles would potentially be distributed in hard copy. All proceeds would be split between the three groups involved, though the actual split is unknown, and those who worked on the title would be properly credited. The first titles are slated to come out this spring, with a goal of 500-1000 new volumes by the end of the year.[22] While there is some skepticism on the feasibility of the project, Digital Manga, Inc., has a positive reputation with fans.[23] They are also holding off on their own portion of the profit until the books are sold, increasing the credibility of the project.[24] Having spoken with President Sasahara directly prior to the announcement at Yaoi Con 2010 and the next day following, I comfortably state that he's sincerely interested in seeing this idea work to the benefit of all – the publishers, Digital Manga, the scanlators, and especially, the fans.[25] It is perhaps the greatest bridge between my previous articles and what could be a major part of the future of digital publishing in the manga industry. Digital Manga, Inc., as could be suggested by its name, has truly been at the forefront of digital publishing for the manga industry. They publish on Kindle, and were the first US manga publisher to publish for the Nook.[26] The previously mentioned eManga website is successfully running and hosting from publishers other than Digital Manga, Inc., and its imprints.

For those fans hoping for something a bit more comprehensive from the Japanese side of the manga industry, 37 Japanese publishers are stepping forward with a North American manga site tentatively called J Manga Portal. The site would digitally distribute the manga owned by the publisher participants, which include Akita Shoten, Kadokawa Shoten, Kodansha, Sheisha, and Shogakukan.[27] The full version of the site is planned for 2011. The site will

---

[22] Cha, Kai-Ming. "DMP Launches the Digital Manga Guild." *Publishers Weekly.* 7 Dec. 2010. Web. <http://www.publishersweekly.com/pw/by-topic/digital/content-and-e-books/article/45433-dmp-launches-the-digital-manga-guild.html>.

[23] Alverson, Brigid. "Digital Manga's Bold Move." *Robot 6*. Comic Book Resources, 9 Nov. 2010. Web. <http://robot6.comicbookresources.com/2010/11/digital-mangas-bold-move/>.

[24] Alverson, Brigid. "Willing to Work on Spec? Digital Manga Has a Job for You!" *Robot 6*. Comic Book Resources, 1 Nov. 2010. Web. <http://robot6.comicbookresources.com/2010/11/willing-to-work-on-spec-digital-manga-has-a-job-for-you/#more-60913>.

[25] Sasahara, Hikaru. "Yaoi Con 2010." Personal interview. 1 Nov. 2010.

[26] Alverson, Brigid. "DMP Launches Manga for the Nook." *Robot 6*. Comic Book Resources, 14 Dec. 2010. Web. <http://robot6.comicbookresources.com/2010/12/dmp-launches-manga-for-the-nook/>.

[27] The other publishers include *Akaneshinsha, ASCII Media Works, East Press, Ichijinsha, Enterbrain, Inc., Oakla Publishing Co., Ltd., Ohzora Publishing Co. , Gakken, Kasakura Shuppansha, Gentosha Comics, Inc., Jitsugyo no Nihon Sha, Ltd., June-Net, Shogakukan-Shueisha Production,*

occasionally offer free manga and other incentives.[28] If the materials for the North American portal are posted translated, this could be a major contender for the best online option for reading manga. However, whether this would be downloadable, like the Apple Apps or Kindle books, is unclear.

It is difficult to say where the digital publishing industry is going, but the educated guess would say everywhere and anywhere. With digital comics and manga expected to grow significantly while print purchases decline and bookstores struggle, publishers will need to jump on the digital bandwagon before it is too late. I see more titles being released in ePub (open e-book format) and in specialized formats for the major e-reader contenders (Kindle, Nook, iPad). Soon, the digital library will outgrow the print library for manga fans and adaptation will become a must. While I enjoy a good book in my hands, travelling the world with a suitcase of books is not nearly as convenient as my little Nook. I agree with Kuo-Yu Liang – "I'm a believer in digital." But are the other fans? Time will tell – as will my next article, in April, after Sakura-Con in Seattle.

Shodensha, Shonen Gahosha Co., Shinshokan Publishing, Shinchosha, Takeshobo, Tatsumi Publishing Co., Ltd., Tokuma Shoten, Nihonbungeisha, Hakusensha, Fujimi Shobo, Fusosha, Futabasha, France Shoin, Bunkasha Publishing Co., Ltd., Houbunsha, Magazine House, Media Factory, LEED Publishing Co., Ltd., and Libre Publishing Co., Ltd.

[28] "37 Japanese Publishers to Launch N. American Manga Portal (Update 3)." *Anime News Network.* 12 Nov. 2010. Web. <http://www.animenewsnetwork.com/news/2010-11-12/37-japanese-publishers-to-launch-n-american-manga-portal>.

The Digital Frontier of Manga Part II

Nicole Nowlin
Berglund Student Fellow, Pacific University

In my previous article, [1] I discussed the state of the manga industry and the various planned, successful, or failed avenues of digital publishing of manga as they can be seen today. The question remains, though, as to whether digital manga is truly the next generation as seen by those who read it. A blog post highlights an interesting story about just that topic, following a moderated panel at the Asia Arts Festival at the University of Kentucky:

> *I chatted a bit more with the panelists (one a soon-to-graduate senior, the other a freshman) and the topic somehow swerved to the manga industry, its travails, and its push to make a market for more esoteric, alternative manga (which for all intents and purposes mostly means "not BESM-standard").*
>
> *After hearing this, the freshman subsequently asked "So, like, are they trying to make it cool to read print manga?" at which both I and the graduating senior goggled for a moment before going "what the hell are you on about?"*
>
> *Apparently, in his high school, it was seen as uncool to read print manga. I didn't find out then why it was particularly considered uncool, although the perpetual-behindness of licensed releases may have been a factor, as well as a certain sense borrowed from underground aesthetics that licensed titles may have "sold out" or were otherwise "too mainstream". It's also interesting to note that the act of "reading manga" itself apparently wasn't considered uncool. Just reading print manga.* [2]

Ironically, it seems the younger generations aren't as adverse to adapting to digital media as those more familiar and entrenched in the manga industry, such as fans who started prior to or during the manga boom in the 2000's. A lot has changed in the manga industry over the years, even prior to the growth of digital media. Matt Thorn, a veteran translator now with *Fantagraphics*, has many

---

[1] http://bcis.pacificu.edu/journal/article.php?id=787

[2] One Great Turtle. "Print Manga Is so Square Hepcat." Web log post. The Library of Babel II. 19 Nov. 2010. Web. http://bibliotaku.tumblr.com/post/1620097773/print-manga-is-so-square-hepcat.

opinions on the changes in the industry. Most come back to the significant drop in translator pay. He lists his "top price [at] $17 per page," while *Tokyopop*, one of the biggest publishers in the industry, hired enthusiasts at $3 per page for what Matt Thorn refers to as "not even close to a living wage." This change in payment created a change in manga price and quality, perhaps leading to some of the misconceptions vocalized by the oblivious freshman in the introductory blog post, but also leading to the lower more affordable prices paid today. Scanlators do the same work for free with the argument that it is sometimes even better quality; *Tokyopop* paid little for their work, which helped depress wages industry-wide.

Now, Digital Manga Guild is combining the two for a profit sharing agreement. It appears the next logical step in the manga industry. [3] Also, *Tokyopop*, despite being one of the two seeming giants of manga publishing, folded last week, possibly as a result of Borders' bankruptcy. [4] Borders was a major seller of the company's publications.

Tokyopop was one of the first on the digital scene with its iPhone app, [5] and their loss is a major shaker for manga fans. Meanwhile, the Digital Manga Guild is revving up exceedingly fast, "with over 1,100 members joining to take part in this manga community initiative." [6]

President Sasahara is finalizing contracts for translation and localization groups, with files to be sent immediately. Files were received from Tokyo, and work is

[3] Alverson, Brigid. "Quote of the Day | Matt Thorn on Tokyopop's Race to the Bottom." Robot 6. Comic Book Resources, 22 Apr. 2011. Web. 26 Apr. 2011.http://robot6.comicbookresources.com/2011/04/quote-of-the-day-matt-thorn-on-tokyopops-race-to-the-bottom/.

[4] Thorn, Matt. "The TokyoPop Effect." Web log post. Generic Blog. 22 Apr. 2011. Web. 26 Apr. 2011. http://matt-thorn.com/wordpress/?p=495.

[5] Chavez, Ed, Michael Gombos, and Marco Pavia. "The Manga Industry Speaks: Taking Stock in Tough Times." Interview by David Brothers. ComicsAlliance. 20 Aug. 2010. Web. http://www.comicsalliance.com/2010/08/20/the-manga-industry-speaks-taking-stock-in-tough-times/.

[6] "Digital Manga Guild Acquires First 487 Titles." Anime News Network. 21 Mar. 2011. Web. 26 Apr. 2011. http://www.animenewsnetwork.com/press-release/2011-03-21/digital-manga-guild- acquires-first-487-titles.

expected to start this season for potential summer releases. The finished manga will be placed online first at *eManga* (http://www.emanga.com), Digital Manga's portal site, and then hopefully expanded to other platforms such as Nook, Kindle, and iPad. The portal is the main stream of digital revenue for Digital Manga Publishing (DMP), as they own the site, with the Kindle coming in second. However, the Nook, despite having far fewer titles than the Kindle (80 versus 200), is nearly as profitable as the Kindle. Kindle also has high fees for digital manga due to the increased file size of images, but President Sasahara insists it is a cost of doing business. Appropriateness for the iPad and iPhone must also be considered, as there are content restrictions on those devices that eliminate the publication of much of DMP's yaoi (boys love) titles.

Further hope is to have the material available regardless of region, so that one book published in English can be distributed in any English speaking country, widening the consumer range. Generally, licenses are as region specific as DVD codes. Furthermore, the project hopes to become multilingual, rather than just Japanese to English. The potential impact of the Guild is significant. In Japan, the cell phone has grown to be a major source for manga viewing, prompting Japanese publishers to relax some of their concerns with regards to approving digital content. President Sasahara says the PC has had less of an impact than the cell phone in Japan, and publishers are realizing more money can be made through digital content. This can smooth the way for a rapid increase in digital publication of manga. [7] At present, "online sales [of printed manga] via sites like Amazon... are a fraction of retail sales, so the manga industry is still very much reliant on brick-and-mortar stores." [8] With the recent shakeups between Borders and *Tokyopop*, this could change as fewer bookstores carry big selections and more publishers find a need for lower cost digital production.

Currently, the fans still have some concerns over how digital publishing will work out in the long run. As it is such a new opportunity, aside from the promise of the Digital Manga Guild, it is hard to determine the results. I had the opportunity to bring up this topic at Sakura Con, an anime convention in Seattle, WA, over Easter weekend. During the panel in which I presented, I asked for feedback on various aspects of digital manga publishing. The room held approximately 30-40 people, but only a handful had an iPad, Kindle, or Nook for digital reading. The Kindle user was generally pleased with the experience, while another had no idea that he could get manga on the Kindle in the first place. The

---

[7] Alverson, Brigid. "Digital Manga Guild Ramps Up Quickly With New Licenses." Publishers Weekly. 12 Apr. 2011. Web. 26 Apr. 2011. http://www.publishersweekly.com/pw/by-topic/digital/content-and-e-books/article/ 46849-digital-manga-guild-ramps-up-quickly-with-new-licenses.html.

[8] shaan. "Tokyopop's Senior Editor On Why Series Go On Hiatus." Siliconera. 26 Feb. 2011. Web. 26 Apr. 2011. http://www.siliconera.com/2011/02/26/tokyopops-senior-editor-on-why-series-go-on- hiatus/.

complaint for the Nook was the lack of varied titles, as there is essentially only Vampire Hunter D and yaoi titles released by DMP. This is likely to broaden in the near future, depending on the success of the Digital Manga Guild.

Concerns expressed were backups of files – for example, if your library is on your digital device and your child drops it in the toilet, then what? Backups were a clear concern. There are digital libraries online in most cases, which is important. The Nook allows you to access any file you purchased through Barnes & Noble at any time, (As does the Kindle for Amazon . com purchases) and both have applications for reading on your phone or computer. Also, as fans are very fond of sharing or passing on titles to others, not having a resale option for unwanted texts was frustrating for some. There is likely to be a lack of cross-platform sharing, such as between the Nook and Kindle, because of proprietary file formats.

Furthermore, online viewing was a concern as it meant the reader never actually owned anything directly – company gone, content gone. This is obviously a concern with the recent loss of *Tokyopop*, so platforms like *eManga* and *Square Enix* weren't well favored by fans in the discussion. [9] *eManga.com* allows readers to rent for 72 hours or buy the manga, but the content is held on the company's website, rather than on the reader's computer or other device. There are plans to close down the rental system in favor of permanent purchase, and there is discussion of offering discounts on the print edition for those who previously purchased the digital edition. [10]

There was dissention regarding whether print would die, and the general consensus was that there woud be a decrease in it as the mainstream method of reading and an increase in small publishers fitting into niche markets. Used books would continue to be important in the case of reading. There was an attendee from a non-profit that provides books to low-income populations in rural school districts, including Native American reservations, and she says she cannot keep a box of manga when she brings them. They're all gone quickly. So for those who replace physical books with e-manga, there will always be a need by those who can't be provided a Kindle or Nook, but can be provided a physical book. A $5000 grant will buy a lot of discounted manga from a used book store, but not so many Kindles or Nooks. Another attendee, a member of the U.S. Coast Guard, made an excellent suggestion – follow the new trend in DVDs of offering a

[9] Nowlin, Nicole. "The Digital Age: EManga." Sakura Con 2011. Washington State Convention and Trade Center, Seattle, WA. 23 Apr. 2011. Panel Presentation.

[10] Alverson, Brigid. "Digital Manga Guild Ramps Up Quickly With New Licenses." Publishers Weekly. 12 Apr. 2011. Web. 26 Apr. 2011.http://www.publishersweekly.com/pw/by-topic/digital/content-and-e-books/article/ 46849-digital-manga-guild-ramps-up-quickly-with-new-licenses.html.

digital copy for a little bit more. This could supplement the interest in digital media and provide a transition point from print to digital. [11]

Such a transition could go in either direction, like President Sasahara's proposed discount on print editions for digital users, or providing a digital edition with the purchase of a print edition as suggested by the panel attendee. Interestingly, President Sasahara views print and digital as complementary rather than competitive, as seems to be the attitude of other publishers. "There are definitely two different types of customers," he said, "light and heavy users. Heavy users always want to buy the print edition; light users want to read the manga once and not keep it on their bookshelves. Just running print editions to me is like a handicap. We want to cater to both types of customers." [12] For books initially released in digital format, popular titles could see a physical print run to appease the fans that do prefer the book in hand with its new-book, just-shrink-wrapped smell.

At the end of my last article, I mused that print would decline, digital would rise, and adaptation to digital would become necessary to keep up. I don't think I was wrong, nor do I think the fans disagreed. Digital is on the rise, though where it will go we still don't know. It will be important to keep watch, especially on the rising star that is the Digital Manga Guild. President Sasahara will push digital forward, as he said, "It's important you feel comfortable and confident about the project and stay with us for five or ten years, and have your kids join the DMG ten years later." [13] An admirable sentiment, but the person who truly ends my article is a fan of manga and a member of the Digital Manga Guild:

> *I love our president's and the rest of DMG's passion to get this project up and running. If I could, I would happily do this all for free just to see it really thrive. I'm just surprised no one's ever thought of it before, because it's an excellent idea! I can't wait to get started. :'D* [14]

---

[11] Nowlin, Nicole. "The Digital Age: EManga." Sakura Con 2011. Washington State Convention and Trade Center, Seattle, WA. 23 Apr. 2011. Panel Presentation.

[12] Alverson, Brigid. "Digital Manga Guild Ramps Up Quickly With New Licenses." Publishers Weekly. 12 Apr. 2011. Web. 26 Apr. 2011.http://www.publishersweekly.com/pw/by-topic/digital/content-and-e-books/article/ 46849-digital-manga-guild-ramps-up-quickly-with-new-licenses.html.

[13] Kokiden, and Doodlelover. "Re: Teleconference Report." Web log comment. Digital Manga. 26 Feb. 2011. Web. 26 Apr. 2011.http://www.digitalmanga.com/forums/viewtopic.php?f=56&t=1533.

[14] Kokiden, and Doodlelover. "Re: Teleconference Report." Web log comment. Digital Manga. 26 Feb. 2011. Web. 26 Apr. 2011. http://www.digitalmanga.com/forums/viewtopic.php?f=56&t=1533.

We've reached just the tip of the mountain for what digital manga publishing can and will become in this industry, and just as the guild member says, "I can't wait to get started."

The End of Sound Slavery

Jake Fischer
Berglund Student Fellow, Pacific University

The Internet has had a huge eaffect on music, completely changing its typical patterns and paths of circulation. It has given much more power to the artist, and taken power away from record labels. Artists speak their true voice on recordings they make themselves ("mixtapes") over which the record labels have no say, and the Internet allows them to spread these to anyone in the world who has access to a computer. Social networking websites, such as Myspace, have given artists the ability to promote themselves without having to pay for CDs and radio play. Listeners are able to download albums faster than they could have listened to them, making digital sales more and more popular. This has led to artists selling their own music online, and finding more ways to challenge major labels. In short, the integration of the Internet into the music business has taken controlling power away from record company executives, and given it to the artists who make the music.

Arguably, the most significant way record labels affect the music they put out is by legally taking "creative control". Without creative control, artists often find themselves unable to release the music as they want it. Record labels try to ensure that the music will sell. Artists are unable to truly represent themselves, as they have to represent the label. For example, the rapper Nas wanted to release an album called "Nigger", believing it would aid in reducing the hateful meaning behind the word. Although he had been a loyal and successful artist, his record label Def Jam forced him to change the title, because they did not hold the same views. This shows just one of many instances of record labels changing artists' messages in their music. It can vary from blocking an artist's album from release to forcing them to insert songs they normally wouldn't on a particular album.

People buy music to hear the artist, not the record label, but what they truly hear is often a watered-down version. Grandmaster Flash, one of the creators of Hip Hop, explains the process as this, "Let's say (we) have two record compan[ies] which I'll call 'Company Left' and 'Company Right'. Let's say Company Left has an artist with a hit record. Company Right would rather come up with a record that sounds like Company Left as opposed to allowing the creative flow of the artist to come up with something" (Davey D).

Companies make artists create songs that sound similar to previous hits. The beauty of art is found in each artist's unique vision of his craft, and conforming them to a set of rules, turns an art into a science, which contradicts art's creative

nature. Grandmaster Flash believes "We can talk about just about anything lyrically. We can even sing off key, but if it's produced properly it can be a hit. What has happened is that there's just too much of one particular subject matter being talked about" (Davey D). Overstressing one area wastes away the rest. Artists create music in the other subject areas, but they remained unsigned by records labels that search for clones of the last big hit.
The Internet gives these artists a portal to the world, the ability to show their art to everybody, without paying radio stations to play the songs, without pretending to be somebody they aren't. They can record a song and immediately upload it to their Myspace or Soundclick page where fans can listen without having to wait for CDs to be made and sent to radio stations or stores. The Internet creates a digital copy that can be copied an infinite amount of times for free and does not need physical CDs to be heard.

Originally, if an artist wanted to release a song or an album there needed to be a hard copy. Records, cassettes, or even CDs cost money to make, and a typical artist could barely afford to make enough for their local area. No artist could gain nationwide popularity on their own, because they could not afford to make sufficient hard copies, let alone advertise.

It was here that record companies came into the picture. They take an artist they believe to be marketable, and in exchange for most of the profits and creative control, they pay for promoting the artist and pressing CDs. For all extents and purposes, the musicians are hired by the record labels, rather than helped. When artists get into arguments with a label, the label can usually do what they want with the music. Grandmaster Flash even had a song released under his name without him knowing anything about it.

> *"Who said that?" I ask him. He points at the radio. "New Grandmaster Flash jam." Can't be. Nobody told me. Morton Berger said they can't use my name until our case settles. I think it must be some kind of mistake. I ask the kid to show me the cassette tape. The kid ain't lying. Sugar Hill Records "White Lines" (Sylvia Robinson/Melvin Glover) Grandmaster Flash and the Furious Five (Ritz).*

The labels view artists as temporary employees, only kept as long as they remain profitable. These labels give the artists money to make an album that the label must approve and have a final say on. Once the album is released, the labels take most of the profit, giving the rest to the artists to be paid right back to the labels for borrowing the original album production money, the advance. If the album does not sell, the artist falls into debt, unable to pay the labels back for the album they were told to make. Such a business structure completely ruins the art, turning it from an artist's creative vision into a product specifically designed by the label to replicate previous hits.

Without the need to press hard copies, artists can release digital copies online free of charge. Rappers often release mixtapes, collections of music similar to albums, but not endorsed by record labels or having a copyright. They were originally used as a means for new artists to promote themselves to get noticed by major labels. These were spread locally, sold to offset the production costs, but their main use was to spread the artist's music. Once signed, artists release mixtapes to distribute songs to the fans that the label would not release. Mixtapes have served as a counter to the major labels' controlling nature, and the Internet has allowed them to be spread easily. This eliminates the need to go through the label and the result is unadulterated music directly from the artists. Mixtapes have many special qualities but:

> *First and foremost is its appeal to the freedom of speech; as the tape was used two decades ago for artistic expression, it is still used today for the same reason. As the demand of the streets and the demand of the labels differs in most cases, mixtapes are solely dropped for the streets, allowing artists to put out whatever they want to, without label's interference (Jasarevic).*

The Internet has also created new ways for the artists to get these mixtapes to a much larger group. Myspace led the way for music promotion through social networking. Artists create a page where they can upload music for Myspace users to listen to. This makes word of mouth advertising much easier, as Internet users can listen to music online without downloading or purchasing anything. "A kid in Warsaw can copy the newest tape on the day of its online release, as can a kid in Zambia or Venezuela" (Jasarevic). Before, bands had to physically tour in an order to spread their music. Scott Schoenbeck, bass player for the band, Dashboard Confessional, says artists used to gain more fans through "Touring, touring, touring... as well as networking and creating your own sense of community around music" (interview via e-mail to the author, November 25th, 2010). With the Internet, networking has become much easier, and online forums enable bands to create a community that can follow their career very easily. The difficulties of promotion and production were the main factor in the development of record labels, and without this they lose a great amount of their leverage.

Jadakiss once said in his song "Why?": "Why is the industry designed to keep the artist in debt?" (Jadakiss). His loss of faith in the industry was probably influenced greatly by the concept of advances:

> *The money which a label pays to an artist to sign and record an album is called an 'advance'. However, as this article will point out, an advance is similar to a loan and thus it has to be paid back, or 'recouped', from the artist's royalties. In other words, the advance has to be paid back in full before the artist sees any money (McLane).*

With this loan system, labels have very little risk. If an album tanks, the artist makes no money and finds himself in debt to the label. If the album is a huge success, the label makes millions while the artist makes a small percentage, after paying back the label. "For every $1,000 in music sold, the average musician makes $23.40" (Jefferson). This assumes there are four musicians in a band, so in total $93.60 is given to the artists that the label signed. The study also shows that the label immediately pockets $0.63 of every $1 the record makes, or $630.00 per thousand.

Unless an artist sells a huge number of records, they are very unlikely to see much, if any money. According to the latest Nielsen research, "only 2.1 percent of the albums released in 2009 sold even 5,000 copies -- that's just 2,050 records out of nearly 100,000" (Jefferson). With a system like that, there was a very poor outlook for those pursuing a career in music. Now, with the ability to sell digital music, artists can sell their work directly to the audience, without the middleman. While digital sales have not passed CD sales, by keeping a much larger percentage of the profit, artists can control their own destiny, and reap much more of the benefits of success.

As a result of the impact of the Internet, record labels began to lose profits, so they thought of a new way to control the artists, called a 360 deal. "The 360 deal is a new kind of provision in a contract that enables the record company to receive a major cut in all of the artist's sources of income, including touring, merchandise and publishing" (Kolmel). One example given is a typical deal by the record company Atlantic. They offer $200,000 to new artists in exchange for 30% of all income, including shows and endorsements. The company then gains control of those aspects of the artist as well, choosing tour dates, destinations, and merchandising. Even worse, there are often clauses in the contracts requiring that the money be paid back to the record company if the artist does not bring in enough money. If the artist does make it big, $200,000 will be far less than 30% of his profits.

Typical artists receive around 13% of album royalties (before repaying the record labels album production costs), and although 360 deal artists receive around 30%, album sales get worse and worse every year, which negates the higher percentage. These deals put artists in a tough position. The deals take almost a third of their income if they make it big, and they lose all their money if they do not. Here, mixtapes again come into play.

Artists are much less often grabbed off of streets and made popular than was formerly the case. But they can now gain strong fan bases before being signed, resulting in more leverage in their contracts. One rapper, Papoose, had such a large fan base that he was able to negotiate 1.5 million dollars in advance money, as well as several important clauses. The most important allowed him to take his advance money and recorded album and leave the label after they decided to put his album on hold.

> *When we did the deal we made sure that clause was in the contract. When it came to the point that they started...leaning more and more toward putting me on the shelf and dropping my album whenever they feel like, we contacted our attorneys to exercise that option in our contract...I got signed by the owner of Jive. The A&R's and all the other people were hating because I didn't go through them. They only eat by bringing in talent off the street then milking the talent like a cow (Hines).*

Due to his reputation, Papoose was able to deal with the owner of the record label, rather than the low ranked workers who all take their fees out of the contract. He was able to create his album on his own, and when the label decided they wanted to hold his album, he left with his money and his music.

Scott Schoenbeck believes "bands have to really work these days and get out and play live nowadays to promote themselves...which I think is good" (personal interview by e-mail, November 25th, 2010). Record labels do not want to take as many risks, due to decreased record sales, so artists have to build a reputation in order to get signed. This leads to artists having much better chances of succeeding, rather than failing to sell and falling into debt. They can also use their larger reputations to negotiate favorable contracts, as Papoose did. Artists can follow paths like these to ensure they do not become slaves to a label.

Entrepreneurism has grown among artists since the use of the Internet, especially with the "do-it-yourself attitude", which is encouraged through self-advertising and distribution. Artists are also learning to focus more on touring and merchandising to make money. These ventures vary from shoes to clubs or even professional sports teams. Artists are beginning to use music to develop fame, and then use the fame to make more money, by putting their name on products.

Jay-Z is the epitome of artist turned entrepreneur. After he became one of rap's most famous artists, he immediately began building his resume by starting up companies with his name and selling them. From the common (record labels, clothing lines) to the uncommon (sports bars, hotels, beauty products, alcoholic beverages) he has taken part in more business ventures than most businessmen ever will, yet he still releases albums to stay relevant and popular (Curan). He has developed a path to success that will gain him more and more followers as music sales continue to decline. When it comes down to it, people buy music for the name of the artist, not the name of the label, and this has become a much greater advantage due to the Internet permitting artists to become businessmen and market themselves.

The Internet has given much greater power to artists. Now artists are relying less and less on labels as a source of income. They can develop a name for themselves through Internet promotion, and gain a solid fan base before going to the labels. This helps them become partners with the labels rather than employees. They can control their own ventures outside of album sales, and become successful on their own terms. They have also gained the ability to pass their unadulterated music to fans through online mixtapes as well. Without the Internet, they would still be under the control of record company executives, and continue to be held in place while making those companies billions. The development of the Internet has set the path for the future of music, and in the next decade we will see how far it truly goes.

References

Curan, Catherine. "Jay-Z's 99 Problems – NYPOST.com." *New York News | Gossip |Sports | Entertainment | Photos* – New York Post. Web. 22 Nov. 2010.http://www.nypost.com/p/news/business/jay_NJOKUMG51yyYswtQo2zrJL/0.

Davey D. "1996 Interview W/ Grandmaster Flash by Davey D." *Davey D's Hip-Hop Corner: The News Source For The Hip-Hop Generation*. Web. 22 Nov. 2010.http://www.daveyd.com/interviewgmflashchronicle.html.

Hines, Haaron. "Papoose: Dream On | Rappers Talk Hip Hop Beef & Old School Hip Hop | HipHopDX." *For New Hip Hop Music, Hip Hop News & All Things Rap & Hip Hop |HipHopDX*. 7 Oct. 2009. Web. 27 Oct. 2010.http://www.hiphopdx.com/index/interviews/id.1420/title.papoose-dream-on.

Jadakiss. "Why?". Kiss of Death. Ruff Ryders, Interscope, 2004.
Jasarevic, Mina. "Disposable Arts: The Evolution Of The Mixtape | Rappers Talk Hip Hop Beef & Old School Hip Hop | HipHopDX." *For New Hip Hop Music, Hip Hop News & All Things Rap & Hip Hop | HipHopDX*. Web. 22 Nov. 2010.http://www.hiphopdx.com/index/interviews/id.1103/title.disposable-arts-the-evolution-of-the-mixtape .

Jefferson, Cord. "The Root Investigates Who Really Gets Paid in the Music Industry."*Home | The Root*. Web. 22 Nov. 2010. http://www.theroot.com/views/how-much-do-you-musicians-really-make?GT1=38002.

Kolmel, Lena. "Record Labels and 360 Deals: What Music Artists Should Know About This New Record Deal." *Suite101.com: Online Magazine and Writers' Network*. 21 Feb. 2010. Web. 27 Oct. 2010. http://www.suite101.com/content/record-labels-and-360-deals-a204630.
McClane, Ben. "Advance." Web. 21 Nov. 2010.
Ritz, David, and Grandmaster Flash. *The Adventures of Grandmaster Flash: My Life, My Beats*. New York: Harlem Moon, 2008. Print.

Politics – Volume 11

DuBoff Law Group, LLC. – *Is Your Business Complying with Website and Email Laws?* http://bcis.pacificu.edu/interface/?p=216

Is Your Business Complying with Website and Email Laws?

THE DuBoff LAW GROUP, LLC

We wrote the book on small business law.

Many small businesses aren't aware of the laws regulating their electronic presence. This alert covers just a few of the legal issues that may arise in connection with your company's website and commercial emails.

While privacy policies are not generally required for websites, if your site has one, it is important that you comply with it. Also remember that you cannot retroactively make your privacy policies less restrictive. If you collect information under an older, more restrictive policy, you cannot then use that information simply by changing your privacy policy and claiming that the new applies to material previously collected. All policy changes should apply only to the future. That is, only information you collect after a policy change can be used in accordance with the new policy; information collected before the policy change must be used in accordance with the old policy.

You are required to have a privacy policy on your site if your website is targeted to kids under 13, or if you are knowingly collecting personal information from kids under 13. That policy must comply with the Children's Online Privacy Protection Act (COPPA). With few exceptions, you also need to be sure that you obtain verifiable parental consent before collecting personally identifiable information from children under the age of 13. Note that COPPA applies to social networks and mobile apps as well as to websites. More information about how to comply with COPPA can be found at: http://business.ftc.gov/privacy-and-security/children%E2%80%99s-online-privacy

Another very important law is the CAN-SPAM Act, which requires those who send commercial emails to have a way recipients can opt out of receiving those emails in the future. When you send emails, do you have an opt-out link? If so, does it work? This law has other requirements as well. You can obtain more information about the CAN-SPAM act at:
http://business.ftc.gov/documents/bus61-can-spam-act-compliance-guide-business

Please feel free to http://www.dubofflaw.com/ if you have any questions about the above issues or other legal issues relating to your website and marketing emails.

Social Media – Volume 11

Erin C. Murphy & Tamara E. Tasker – *Lost in a Crowded Room: A Correlational Study of Facebook & Social Anxiety*
http://bcis.pacificu.edu/interface/?p=395

Jeff Cain – *Social Media: Tool for Social Good or Aid to Slacktivism?*
http://bcis.pacificu.edu/interface/?p=484

Lost in a Crowded Room: A Correlational Study of Facebook & Social Anxiety

Erin C. Murphy, M.S.

Tamara E. Tasker, Psy. D.
Assistant Professor

School of Professional Psychology, Pacific University

Introduction

Social Phobia is a frequently disabling condition characterized by fear of embarrassment and judgment in social and/or performance situations that manifests in different ways.[1] Individuals may avoid very specific tasks, such as public speaking or engaging in motor behaviors, such as eating, drinking, or writing, in the presence of others. Additionally, these individuals may fear overt, physiological "clues" to their anxiety, including blushing, stammering, or trembling. Avoidance of these social and performance situations often leads to impairment in occupational and social settings, negatively impacting the individual. Such fear and impairment leads to marked distress in these individuals as they withdraw from social and occupational settings. [2]

With the advent of the internet and social networking sites, individuals with social phobia now have a method by which to avoid face-to-face communication while still interacting with others. Communication done via computer allows the individual more control over the situation than face-to-face communication. For example, individuals can slow conversation, allowing them to think through, edit, and delete thoughts if desired. They can get up and leave the computer (and thus the conversation) if they wish. Additionally, overt physiological symptoms of blushing, sweating, trembling, and voice quivering are safely hidden from view. [2]

A social networking site is a website that allows individuals to create a profile and a list of other users ("friends") with whom to converse and share

---

[1] Turk, C. L., Heimberg, R. G., & Hope, D. A. (2003). Social anxiety disorder. In D. Barlow (Ed.) Clinical handbook of psychological disorders: A step-by-step treatment manual, Third edition, (pp. 114-153). New York: The Guilford Press.
[2] Schulz, S. M., Meuret, A. E., Loh, R., & Hofmann, S. G. (2007). Social Phobia. In M. Hersen and J. C. Thomas (Eds.) Handbook of clinical interviewing with adults, First edition, (pp.223-237). Los Angeles: SAGE Publications.

information. [3] In 2004, Mark Zuckerberg, a Harvard University student, created Facebook, a social networking site that allowed students to connect with their peers. [4] By 2006, the social networking site was extended beyond students to include anyone over the age of 13 with an email address. On Facebook, an individual's profile has a predetermined layout that includes a picture of the individual, a "wall" on which friends may post comments, weblinks, a list of the individual's friends, and photos that either the individual or his or her friends have posted. The user can determine privacy of his or her profile, thus limiting it to only friends or leaving it public. Currently, the site boasts over 400 million active users, with an average of 500 billion minutes spent on the site per month. [4]

Facebook's tremendous popularity has prompted researchers to study the appeal of social networking. Recent studies have focused upon topics ranging from broad characteristics of the typical site user to the use of these sites in the treatment of mental illness. One area that has gained some attention is the *rich-get-richer* hypothesis, which states that those who are extroverted are most likely to benefit from social networking sites. [5] Thus far, there have been mixed findings with respect to this hypothesis leading to declarations that these sites are both helpful and hindering. [6] [7]

The current study will examine the relationship between Facebook use and social anxiety. More specifically, there are two hypotheses. First, it is hypothesized that there will be a significant, positive relationship between time spent on Facebook and scores on a social anxiety scale. Secondly, it is hypothesized that scores on this measure will have a significant, positive relationship with individuals who find online communication easier. This item will be coded such that higher scores will denote the degree to which online communication is easier than face-to-face communication. In sum, it is hypothesized that as time spent on Facebook increases, and perceived ease of online communication increases, social anxiety scores will also increase.

---

[3] Boyd, D. M., & Ellison, N. B. (2007). Social network sites: Definition, history, and scholarship. Journal of Computer-Mediated Communication, 13(1), article 11.
[4] Facebook, 2010
[5] Sheldon, P. (2008). The relationship between unwillingness-to-communicate and students' Facebook use. Journal of Media Psychology, 20(2), 67-75.
[6] Baker, J. R., & Moore, S. M. (2008). Blogging as a social tool: A psychosocial examination of the effects of blogging. Cyberpsychology & Behavior, 11(6), 747-749.
[7] Kramer, N. C., & Winter, S. (2008). Impression management 2.0: The relationship of self-esteem, extraversion, self-efficacy, and self-presentation within social networking sites. Journal of Media Psychology, 20(3), 106-116.

Method

- Participants

Participants within the present study were recruited using flyers, email, and posts on the primary researcher's personal Facebook page. Individuals completed the online survey using SurveyMonkey and were presented with a copy of Informed Consent explaining their rights as a participant. Participation was voluntary and participants were able to exit the survey at any time. No compensation was provided for participation. Participants indicated they were over 18 years of age and had a Facebook account. A total of 388 surveys were completed and analyzed.

- Measures

Within the present study, the following assessments were presented to each research participant:

Social Anxiety. The Liebowitz Social Anxiety Scale, Self-Report (LSAS) – a 48-item questionnaire – was utilized as a measure to assess 4 subcategories: performance fear, social fear, performance avoidance, and social avoidance. Additionally, the scale provides scores related to social interaction fear and avoidance, and public performance fear and avoidance. The participants were first asked to rate their fear or anxiety on 24 items on a 4-point Likert-type scale: none, mild, moderate, or severe. Participants were then instructed to rate their avoidance on 24 items using a 4-point Likert-type scale: never, occasionally (1 - 33%), often (33 –67%), or usually (67% -100%). A fear/anxiety score, avoidance score, social score, performance score, and total social anxiety score were then calculated.

Facebook Use. Because an assessment of Facebook use is currently not available, and given the exploratory nature of the study, the researchers created an 18-item questionnaire on basic Facebook use. Items included estimating one's number of friends, identifying uses for Facebook, and estimating time spent on Facebook. A score was coded for each item. For the purposes of the research, two items were analyzed: time spent on Facebook and ease of online communication.

Demographic Questionnaire. Participants provided standard demographic information including sex, age, ethnicity, and current marital status.

Results

A total of 388 surveys were completed. Of these, 74.4% were female, 25.4% were male, and 1 individual chose the option "would rather not say." With regard to ethnicity, 85.9% identified as Caucasian, 6.9% as Asian American, 2.6% as "other," 1.8% as multiracial, 1.3% as Hispanic, 0.8% as "would rather not say," 0.5% as American Indian/Alaskan Native, and 0.3% as Pacific Islander/Native Hawaiian. African American was included as an option, but was not endorsed. The average age of participants was 29 years (M = 29.42, SD = 8.43), with a range of 20 to 60 years of age. The majority of participants were single (47.3%), while 27.7% were married, 19.0% were cohabitating, 3.6% were divorced, 1.3% marked "would rather not say," and 1.0% were separated. Widowed was offered as an option, but was not endorsed.

The researchers were interested in determining if a significant relationship existed between social anxiety scores and Facebook use. Specifically, researchers compared scores on the Liebowitz Social Anxiety Scale (total social anxiety, total social avoidance, total performance anxiety, total performance avoidance, and overall anxiety total), with time spent on Facebook and with ease of online communication. There were two hypotheses: (1) a significant, positive relationship between time spent on Facebook and scores on the Liebowitz Social Anxiety Scale (LSAS), and (2) a significant, positive relationship between ease of online communication and scores on the LSAS.

For the first hypothesis, variables were analyzed using Pearson product moment correlations. Data was collected from 388 completed surveys. Using the Bonferroni approach to control for Type I error across the 5 correlations, a p value of less than .01 (.05/5) was required for significance. The results of the correlational analyses indicated that two of five correlations were statistically significant. There was a significant, positive relationship found between time spent on Facebook and total performance avoidance, $r(388) = .153$. This indicates that time spent on Facebook and performance avoidance vary together. A significant, positive relationship was also found between time spent on Facebook and overall LSAS total, $r(388) = .132$, indicating that these two variables vary together. Relationships between time spent on Facebook and social anxiety, social avoidance, and performance anxiety were not found to be significant.

For the second hypothesis, variables were analyzed using Pearson product moment correlations. Data was collected from 388 completed surveys. Using the Bonferroni approach to control for Type I error across the 5 correlations, a p value of less than .01 (.05/5) was required for significance. The results of the correlational analyses indicated that five of five correlations were statistically significant. There was a significant, positive relationship between ease of online communication and overall LSAS total, $r(388) = .343$, indicating that these two variables vary together. A significant, positive relationship was also found between ease of online communication and social anxiety, $r(388) = .351$. Additionally, a significant, positive relationship was found between ease of online communication and social avoidance, $r(388) = .338$. A significant, positive relationship was found between ease of online communication and performance anxiety, $r(388) = .285$. Finally, a significant, positive relationship was found between ease of online communication and performance avoidance, $r(388) = .275$.

Discussion

The researcher sought to determine if a significant relationship existed between time spent on Facebook and social anxiety, as well as perceived ease of online communication and social anxiety. Indeed, significant, positive relationships were found for each hypothesis. However, the direction of each relationship is unknown. More specifically, the research does not reveal if Facebook use leads to greater social anxiety, or conversely, if social anxiety leads to increased Facebook use. Furthermore, due to the correlational nature of the study, it is unknown if a causal relationship exists and to what extent.

This study sought to build on previous research and offer an interesting look into Facebook use. According to Experian Hitwise, an online intelligence service, Facebook was the most visited website in 2010, ousting Google.com from the top spot, and these numbers are predicted to increase. [8] With use of the popular site

on the rise, it has and will continue to have an effect on people's lives, especially those who have difficulty communicating face-to-face. This study shows that there is in fact a relationship between social anxiety and Facebook use.

As the researcher created the Facebook measure in collaboration with her advisor, the statistical properties are unknown. The measure did not undergo screening, nor was a panel employed to address potential questions or inconsistencies. Additionally, reading level of the questions was not formally addressed. Content of the questions was determined solely by the researcher to address specific research questions. A measure to assess use of social networking sites would lead to increased understanding of the impacts of site use and thus add to the field's knowledge.

Due to the limited scope of the study, some information remains unknown. For example, dual diagnoses were not addressed. While the LSAS assesses for social anxiety and avoidance, the researcher did not address additional diagnoses (e.g. Generalized Anxiety Disorder, Specific Phobia, Avoidant Personality Disorder)

---

[8] Hitwise.com, 2011

that may have confounded the data. In addition, the researcher did not query past or present use of anti-anxiety medications, or participation in individual or group therapies. Such information could have created a more complete picture of individuals' experience of anxiety. Additionally, participant geographic location is unknown. In order to obtain subjects, the researcher recruited through email to her graduate program, fliers posted in the greater Portland area, and an advertisement on the researcher's personal Facebook page; as such, the sample may not be representative of the general population. While the demographic questionnaire assessed ethnicity, the researcher did not query the participant's state or national citizenship. A future study might assess correlations among demographics (e.g. age, ethnicity, gender, and nationality), social anxiety, and use of social networking sites.

As the study was conducted via online survey, it is reliant on the participant's perception of social networking site use, as well as the participant's rating of his/her subjective experience of social anxiety and avoidance (i.e. lack of corroboration of the severity of anxiety with friends or family members).

While many facets of social networking sites as they relate to social anxiety remain unknown, it is clear that a significant, positive relationship exists between social anxiety and both use of these sites and perceived ease of online communication. It will be critical for those studying the phenomenon of social anxiety and internet-based trends to research social networking sites and their effects in order to comprehend and competently treat the disorder.

Social Media: Tool for Social Good or Aid to Slacktivism

Jeff Cain

Adjunct Associate Professor

Department of Pharmacy Practice & Science

Director of Education Technology

College of Pharmacy, University of Kentucky

Some think that social media is a virtual garden in which societal, cultural, and political activism can flourish, but is that truly the case? I will answer that question up front by stating, "Yes, the Web 2.0 world absolutely offers an expanded venue for activism". I have pondered this topic for a while, but one particular case of activism, on the web, captured my attention and prompted me to consider the actual effect of these online activities. As regular users of Facebook will probably recall, in early 2010 many females began changing their Facebook statuses to the name of a color. [1] Not unlike many other things involving females, men everywhere were befuddled with this phenomenon. Eventually the secret code was cracked (or more likely revealed) that the colors referred to a woman's favorite bra color. The point of this online exercise was to increase breast cancer awareness. Did it raise awareness? Maybe just a little bit. Did it give those women who played along a sense of satisfaction that they were doing something "good"? Possibly. Did it accomplish anything tangible with regard to curing or treating breast cancer? Probably not very much.

This phenomenon continued and has been replicated for various other causes. I perceive it to be a little more than the email chain letter promising a substantial donation to [insert cause here] if the email is forwarded to a million people. From personal observation, it appears that the same individuals tend to participate in all of these online activities. What exactly is anyone gaining from this? Is this the best we can do with Facebook? Is this an innovative use of social media to advance a cause or is the platform being reduced to a mere vehicle for "slacktivism". Slacktivism (a slang term fusing "slack" and "activism") is defined loosely as, "activism that requires little effort (and often has little effect) and is mainly designed to make participants feel better about themselves." [2] Do social

---

[1] Carmichael M. What color is your bra? Facebook's pointless underwear protest. Available at: http://www.newsweek.com/blogs/the-human-condition/2010/01/08/what-color-is-your-bra-facebook-s-pointless-underwear-protest.html. Accessed March 20, 2011.

[2] Definition of slacktivism. Available at:http://onlineslangdictionary.com/definition+of/slacktivism. Accessed March 20, 2011.

media provide slacktivists with new opportunities to increase feelings of self value by doing nothing but typing a few words or changing a Facebook profile picture? I surmise that a large number may be doing this just for the entertainment value with no regard for the intended purpose.

My initial thoughts on this matter mirrored others who believe that slacktivism only trivializes issues, does nothing practical, and may become a distraction to real activity. [3] Facebook activism has been described as activism that succeeds to motivate people to do things that people do when they are not willing to make a real sacrifice. [4] What is actually accomplished when someone changes his/her Facebook profile picture to a banner that promotes a cause? Can something that literally takes only a few seconds translate into an action with meaningful results? In spite of the criticisms, at least some people seem to think that these are actually worthwhile activities and that assumptions behind the term "slacktivism" are flawed. [5] Those in that camp believe that small steps such as signing an online petition lead to larger commitments and that the grand sum of all slacktivist activity (I suppose that can be called "slacktivity") can be a catalyst for change because it signals widespread support. "Clicktivism" serves to influence people, change minds, and alter perceptions. [6] On a different level, recent examples from Iran's Green Revolution and Egypt's political uprising demonstrate that the activist voice of common citizens can be amplified through social media, much more than through traditional modes of communication. [7] Similarly, with regard to labor unions, activists have discovered that social media reaches more people faster and cheaper than traditional communication channels. [8]

After researching both sides of the debate, my opinion has been altered, although only slightly. I can reasonably envision how a particular "clicktivist" activity might go viral, garner national attention, and influence decision makers.

---

[3] Schonfeld S. Online 'slacktivism' sparks debate. Available at: http://www.dailypennsylvanian.com/article/online-slacktivism-sparks-debate. Accessed February 15, 2011.

[4] Gladwell M. Small change: Why the revolution will not be tweeted. The New Yorker. Available at: http://www.newyorker.com/reporting/2010/10/04/101004fa_fact_gladwell?currentPage=all. Accessed March 20, 2011.

[5] Paynter R. Slacktivism: Why Snopes got it wrong about Internet petitions. Available at: http:/www.care2.com/causes/trailblazers/blog/slacktivism-why-snopes-got-it-wrong-about-internet-petitions/ . Accessed March 15, 2011.

[6] Smith C. Down with clicktivism! Or not. Available at: http://cheritasmith.com/blog/down-with-clicktivism-or-not/. Accessed March 30, 2011.

[7] Kapin A. Can social media create and spread revolution? Available at: http://www.frogloop.com/care2blog/2011/1/30/can-social-media-create-and-spread-revolution.html. Accessed March 31, 2011.

[8] Parks J. Social media: New tools aid in organizing. Available at: http://blog.aflcio.org/2009/09/29/social-media-new-tools-aid-in-organizing/. Accessed March 20, 2011.

However, I still believe that the majority of Facebook memes and similar popular social media trends, as described earlier, only give the illusion of activism while producing no concrete results. Regardless of the stance taken on this particular issue, the fact of the matter is that social media applications have been developed that take a more practical approach to supporting social good. Ease of communications and virtually cost-free ways to organize groups of individuals make social media an attractive toolset for those deeply involved with advancing a cause. Granted, many of the sites revolve around fundraising, which has its own set of critics who decry that monetary donations are simply another form of slacktivism. However, monetary contributions are tangible and the effects can be noticed and measured.

Examples

Let us forget for a moment the somewhat frivolous nature of Facebook statuses, groups, and fan pages, and consider the other online resources that use a Web 2.0 philosophy to raise awareness, collect donations, and organize events. The number of sites that promote social causes has increased dramatically over the last few years and I am only briefly summarizing a few that represent various purposes and functionality. These utilities range in purpose from organizing and equipping people to advance social causes, to collecting money at a grassroots level, to removing the logistical transaction costs of loans to those in remote regions of the world.

The NetSquared [9] initiative seeks to help non-profit and non-governmental organizations utilize community-empowering social media tools to increase impact and create change. Online communities and tools provide opportunity for collaboration with others, creating/sharing innovative ideas, and to support various activist projects.

GiveForward [10] facilitates online fundraising by providing free, personalized fundraising pages to groups and individuals for whatever cause they are promoting. This site allows individuals and small groups to have access to the same type of online tools that large charitable organizations have. The only cost to the user is a nominal processing fee.
Kiva [11] is a non-profit organization that seeks to alleviate global poverty by connecting people who are willing to fund entrepreneurial activity across the globe. The site facilitates small loans to users in third world and developing countries for the purpose of creating or expanding small business in poverty-stricken areas. Kiva's vision is to create opportunity for all people, even in the most remote regions of the world, to create jobs and provide sustainable

[9] http://netsquared.org
[10] http://www.giveforward.com
[11] http://www.kiva.org

incomes. Kiva users can lend in part or in whole to a project of their choice. Once the loan is paid in full, that money either can be withdrawn or applied to another project.

These three simple examples provide only a glimpse of the potential power of social media to facilitate activism. More sites are being developed every day that permit individuals and organizations to readily connect with potential contributors.

Summary

Social media allows us to connect to virtually anyone and any organization with little to no effort. The ability to become involved with a social cause is literally at the tips of our fingers. The problem is that if we are not careful, we can unwittingly be attracted to slacktivities that make us feel good, but contribute practically nothing to the actual cause.

I implore each of us to critically examine our own response when we receive the request to follow yet another Facebook "meme of the day." Ask the right questions. Is changing our profile photo to a cartoon character really preventing child abuse [12] or is it just a superficial contribution that assuages feelings of guilt? I suggest that the next time you feel the urge to comply with this sort of request that you also seek an opportunity to make a tangible contribution to your cause of choice. We are in an age in which anyone with average computer skills can seek and find ways to contribute to worthwhile activist campaigns. Whether it occurs through organization of others, through advocacy, or through fundraising, surely we can find a way to use social media to improve our world.

---

[12] Banks E. Facebookers changing profile pics to cartoon characters to fight child abuse. Available at: http://mashable.com/2010/12/03/cartoons-facebook-end-violence/. Accessed March 20, 2011.

Technology – Volume 11

Nicole Nowlin – *Barnes & Noble nook Color: User Review*
http://bcis.pacificu.edu/interface/?p=454

Maria Walters – *The Internet: Data with a Purpose*
http://bcis.pacificu.edu/interface/?p=347

Clare Richardson-Barlow – *Kindle Use Abroad*
http://bcis.pacificu.edu/interface/?p=489

Michael Geraci – *Overlays and the Optimal User Experience*
http://bcis.pacificu.edu/interface/?p=255

Greg Orlowsky & Peter Orlowsky – *A Review of the iPad After One Year*
http://bcis.pacificu.edu/interface/?p=409

Barnes & Noble Nook Color: User Review

Nicole Nowlin
Berglund Student Fellow, Pacific University

Thanksgiving 2010 brought a new player to the e-reader market – the Barnes & Noble Nook Color. The market offering of e-reader technology has been growing steadily for the last decade, and was long dominated by the Kindle. Only a partial new player in the market, the Nook Color significantly upgraded its black-and-white e-ink predecessor into a multi-functional entertainment device. This put it above and beyond the Kindle as a useful e-reader. Imagine an iPad crossed with a Kindle – e-reader functionality, an app store, and media entertainment options. Now, eliminate the Kindle's e-ink screen and replace it with a full-color iPad screen, crop the iPad to about Kindle size, and mix the prices for a semi-comfortable $249 price tag. That is the Barnes & Noble Nook Color.

I purchased my Nook in mid-December when it became obvious I had a lot of travelling to do in the spring. An avid reader, it was suddenly obvious I'd be a fool to carry a dozen Sherrilyn Kenyon and Gena Showalter novels on an airplane to three different countries – especially considering I'd finish one such novel in three hours, meaning I'd finish three on a full plane ride. They wouldn't last the month in Asia for which they were needed, or the following week in Europe later in spring. I had a problem, and Barnes & Noble had a solution.

Let me explain first why I chose the Nook Color over the market leading Kindle. I can sum it up in one word: COLOR. This was the first draw of the new Nook (hereafter simply referred to as "Nook"), but the clincher in the Kindle interest coffin was the multi-functionality. I'm a busy person who wants her technology to do everything at once. The Nook is the closest to offer this without paying for an iPad, something I am unwilling to do. On the Nook, I can use the Internet, play music, games, and movies, and read good old-fashioned books. It has become my portable entertainment device.

I will split my examination of the Nook into three parts – pluses, minuses, and suggestions. For the technical specifications, please visit the Nook website (http://www.barnesandnoble.com/nook/). I'll start here with the pluses.

Pluses

As I've stated in my introduction, the biggest "plus" of the Nook is its functionality. I'm able to play music in the background while browsing the Internet, reading a book, or playing a game – or switching between all three. Unlike the first generation iPad, where you could run one app and play music in the background, I can move between multiple activities on the Nook and it handles it just fine. The web browser is simple and allows for multiple windows (no more than six or seven, but I don't consider that a minus). It is compatible with most web-based email systems (Yahoo!, Hotmail, AOL, and other proprietary programs), runs searches easily, allows for downloads, and loads Facebook like a champ (a definite requirement for a socially minded college student).

The Nook runs a version of the Android operating system found on smart phones. With this came the promise of an app store that, while delayed, has finally come to fruition. With the latest system upgrade is a Nook-formatted list of apps just as with any Android phone, and the list keeps growing. Furthermore, the system added an integrated email program, such as on your cell phone, and installed Flash support. The iPad does not yet support Flash, but it was with great excitement that I pulled up a video on a website and had it play with no problems. The cell phone version of YouTube is no longer required.

On the hardware side of things, the touch screen is sensitive and zooms in or out with the closing and opening of fingers, like an iPhone. My brightness is typically set at about 15-20% of the full screen brightness. In daylight, I might increase to 50% or more. When you want it bright, it gets BRIGHT. The volume is comfortably loud enough to place the Nook in a room and let it be your music player as you putter around. Vacuuming drowns everything out, so it certainly can't overcome noisy activities. It isn't designed to be that loud (again, as a personal device, I don't consider this a minus).

The library design for the Nook books and other downloads allows the creation of shelves where you can place the different books. One book can fit multiple shelves – say, an author and a genre. Books you no longer need on your physical device can be archived back to your virtual bookstore on the Barnes & Noble website if it was purchased from there. Third party open-source books, like ePub, have to be deleted from the Nook directly as they're not a part of the Nook system. I've discovered that when you archive a book that is stored on a shelf in your library, you can still see it on the shelf as available for download should you wish to acquire it again. If you remove it from the shelf it appears only under the "Archived" list, and to permanently delete the books you delete them from your virtual library. (You must repurchase the book if you deleted the wrong book).

The Wifi sync works well and downloads without issue, unless you are in China attempting to download a paper on Tiananmen Square. I tried. Check the minuses for the discussion on download restrictions.

Also, any books or applications downloaded to one Nook are downloaded to all other Nooks on the same account. You can have multiple Nooks under one name so that there are no limits to sharing books that two people enjoy. My mother and I are on my account so that we may have access to all of the authors we both read. There is also a share feature that allows you to loan a book to a friend with a Nook for two weeks. During that time, the book is unavailable for you to read, as though you had physically loaned the book to a friend, creating a similar situation with which we may be familiar.

Minuses

For all that I love my Nook, it is hardly perfect. The newest upgrade does address some of my concerns, but not all of them. For example, although the Nook worked well with email and now has an integrated email program, I found that Hotmail could often freeze my web browser, leaving me with no way to move to a new window or back to a previous page, as the menu for the web browser does not work when the page is loading. I'll avoid going to hotmail.com directly now that I can download email into the email interface.

Prior to my purchase of the Nook, I had little familiarity with Android other than through friends' reviews and what I read online. I was disappointed to find, initially, that I couldn't use the full YouTube site nor could I load Netflix or other Flash-based video players. For a multi-functional device that I was hoping to use for a lot of convenient entertainment, it was pretty disappointing. The latest upgrade, to my pleasure, included Flash, and while I did find sites that I could now watch videos on, Netflix Watch Instantly still fails to load. It is not a strong enough system for the Netflix program. Whether this means we need a Netflix Mobile or something similar, or an improvement in the Nook itself, remains to be seen.

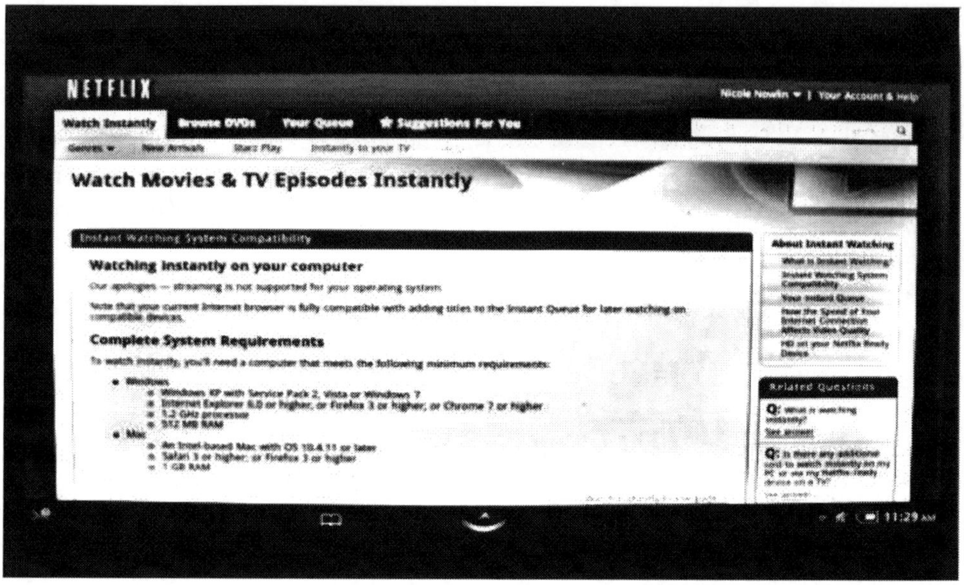

The touch screen is almost overly sensitive at times, with a wake up touch bringing a change in songs on your playlist. This is a slippery slope, as one wants sensitivity and so likely needs to deal with the easy slips. Using Facebook is often easier with the screen horizontal and zoomed, as clicking on “Poke” next to a person’s name in your notifications can take you to the person’s profile rather than the pop up box asking for permission to poke your friend. The links are too small when not zoomed to use easily. Also, when typing online, no cursor appears between letters to show where you are if you must go back and edit. This means deleting and replacing letters with multiple touches to find the right spot, as there are no arrow navigation keys on the virtual touch-screen keyboard either. Also, the screen is not e-ink, nor can it change between the two settings like some tablets, and so is harder on the eyes than a typical e-ink e-reader, like the Kindle.

While I appreciate the library and shelving options for the Nook, when on a downloading spree it is hard to tell what has been categorized or not, as there is no “uncategorized” shelf nor is there a list of shelves next to the book’s information in the full library. Furthermore, when you have two Nooks on one account, archiving a book on one Nook will archive it on the other. This is unfortunately not what I was led to believe when I added my mother to my Nook account so we could share books. We were led to believe we could archive from our own Nooks and it wouldn’t affect the other. Needless to say, much confusion ensued when numerous books disappeared from my screen and later reappeared on hers when I removed them from the archive. I doubt she's all that interested in reading my Japanese manga, but I'd like to keep my access to them. Unfortunately, sharing with friends only works for Nook books and not any book on your Nook, as the publication must go through the Nook system. This makes it a bit harder to share titles from third-party publishers, like niche and independent companies.

While the Wifi sync works, copyright laws don't allow users to purchase while in other countries. Despite my account and billing information being in the US, I couldn't purchase while in China or Japan (and not just the firewall-blocked Tiananmen Square piece). I was informed I could download pieces if someone in the US purchased it through my account. So, downloading is possible while abroad, but purchasing is not. It's a rather strange little paradox, as you get the content either way.

Suggestions

First, let me say I don't regret buying my Nook. I still love it, especially with its new upgrades. However, I would like to see more customization come to it. By customization I mean Barnes & Noble should not expect every Nook in a family to want the same books. While we're sharing many books through one account, archiving on one Nook should not remove it from another. For this, I make the suggestion of an update dialog box that says something like, "Sync Options: Sync All / Select Sync Items" so that you can choose to update everything, or just browse what is newly made available to sync to your Nook, such as new purchases or new applications. Archiving won't affect the other Nook at all, which would certainly be nice when one person finishes a book far earlier than the other. Along those same lines, a method of noting which of your 100 books is uncategorized would be appreciated.

And of course, being very entertainment minded, please allow me to use Netflix on my Nook. The entertainment possibilities are endless (and legal) with Watch Instantly. Some arrangement between Netflix and Barnes & Noble to format Watch Instantly for Nook, or Nook for Watch Instantly, would result in many excited exclamations on my part. I'm sure I'm not the only Nook user who thinks so.
I believe my previous assertion that the Nook Color is a cross between the iPad and the Kindle is appropriate. It's far more useful than the Kindle, but smaller and less expensive than the iPad. I'm curious to see what else they come up with for this platform.

The Internet: Data with a Purpose

Maria Walters
Pacific University Graduate

Adam and Eve ate the apple. Babies grow up. Frankenstein's monster ended up with a mind of his own. Great literature, and great life, is made by people and things that rebel against their maker's wishes and evolve into something more.

This century's greatest invention, the Internet, is evolving, too. Or should we say that the uses for the Internet are changing and growing? Or is it the users? Yes, yes, and yes!

When the Internet was first being dreamt up, more than 20 years ago, it was data for data's sake, a way for scientists to access what others were discovering. It was only a matter of time before a comprehensive, evolving encyclopedia was created. Even e-mail might have seemed like an afterthought.

But as soon as you let humans start using the Internet, things start taking an unpredictable turn.

Connecting with people you already knew was expected, like an updated telephone. Researchers finding other researchers wouldn't have been out of the question, connecting with questions about data. But meeting others online? Growing relationships when your only contact is through a computer connection? Collaborating and trusting one another sight unseen? Inspiring one another? Somehow all of these bits of data flying around have turned into something more.

Inspiration

Of course, self-help books existed long before the Internet did – and some gems contain good advice that has withstood the test of time. But as people began connecting online, the blind could truly lead the blind – and grow together, instead of waiting for an "expert" to take them under their wing. Countless well-known and established blogs were founded when their creators decided to use accountability to a group of strangers to propel them to living out their dreams. And now their stories of success have already spawned other lives to follow suit.

People who never would have met now have a chance to see others living however they want to, inspiring a new round of crazy ideas… and somehow I doubt that it will ever stop.

Here are a few of the goals that people are helping each other achieve on blogs and forums. Many of them are concrete lifestyle changes – totally separate from the worldwide nature of the Internet – but they all boil down to people being able to live their dreams and change their lives. Online, there are always people who are embarking on similar journeys and who are excited to watch you become you, whatever it takes. Plus, there are always those who are ahead of you and can spur you on, and those behind you that you can be a role model for.

Live or travel anywhere

The first users of the Internet probably marveled at the fact that, since computers were connected to the network, one computer could do the same things as another. I'm sure they thought about logging onto computers in other locations and being able to continue their work with the data they stored online.

But now, the theory has been put into practice – people are moving their important data to the cloud so they can access it anywhere, and many people make their livings without always working in the same location. Whether it's working from your laptop at Starbucks across the street or across the world, more people are location independent than realize it.

Bloggers encouraging people to travel include Karol Gajda of Ridiculously Extraordinary[1] and Chris Guillebeau of The Art of Non-Conformity[2]. Chris Guillebeau is even popularizing the concept of travel-hacking – traveling cheaply, especially using frequent flyer miles – and just completed his own book tour through all 50 U.S. states and 13 Canadian provinces.

Make money online

Scams are not the only way to make money online – in fact, there are as many models of selling digital products and services as there are people using the Internet as their marketplace. Digital products include ebooks, videos, and audio that people pay to download and use; services range from being a virtual assistant to a designer to a consultant.

Of course, learning how to earn income online becomes circular quickly: many experts make money online while (or by!) teaching others to do so as well. Good

---

[1] Ridiculously Extraordinary: http://www.ridiculouslyextraordinary.com/
[2] The Art of Non-Conformity: http://chrisguillebeau.com/3x5/

sources of information include Pat Flynn's The Smart Passive Income Blog[3] and Darren Rowse's Problogger[4]. Advertising allows both men to offer their advice for free while still making money from it.

Speak another language

Even online, there are pretty dramatic divisions between people along language barriers. However, the interconnectivity of the Internet also gives us ways to seek out and learn other languages. Benny Lewis writes a blog called Fluent in 3 Months [5] describing his life as a "language hacker" who takes advantage of being location independent to learn languages quickly and well: he has learned 8 languages in 7 years! He says the Internet is an integral part of being able to maintain all those languages.

Live more intentionally

This category could (and probably should) be an article unto itself. In a world where we are sometimes too accustomed to taking orders, doing homework, and being influenced by advertisements, it's really hard to sort through the influences to decide what to do or who to be.

Fortunately, the Internet supplies people who have become more intentional in many areas of their lives, and who are readily supplying encouragement and guidance.

Unfortunately, if you overwhelm yourself with the encouragements to change so many different elements of yourself, it can be hard to change anything. Suddenly, those personal, encouraging influences begin to become background noise like all the other orders that exist in our lives. Before choosing what to change, we need to choose what to consume.

Out there

The real story isn't here – it's in the endnotes, it's out there. Blogs are a great way to get to know and connect with people you can identify with online and all over the world. And they're not part of a textbook, they're a conversation, an edge of the iceberg.

Check out one of these blogs and join the conversation! Or leave a comment below with another inspiring blog!

---

[3] The Smart Passive Income Blog: http://www.smartpassiveincome.com/
[4] Problogger: http://www.problogger.net/
[5] Fluent in 3 Months: http://www.fluentin3months.com/

Kindle Use Abroad

Clare Richardson-Barlow

Whether it's waiting for delayed planes, avoiding bad movies, long cab rides from airports to hotels, or sleepless jet-lagged nights, my Amazon Kindle has more than paid for itself when traveling. It has prevented me from dying of boredom and aided me in work-related tasks I would be unable to otherwise complete.

However, on a recent international trip (from California to China via Japan) I was forced to adapt to using my Kindle abroad, outside of the scope of America's wireless Internet luxury. We all know the effectiveness of Amazon's wireless book within the comfort of our own country, but what is the Kindle's effectiveness elsewhere? Does the Kindle continue to do what its clever marketing promises, or are there international glitches that still need to be solved before jetsetters can justify the investment?

The answer to whether or not the Amazon Kindle remains effective outside of the United States is two part: yes and no. This review will focus on Asia, as that is where I recently traveled, aided by my trusty electronic book.

At the outset let me establish that all of my previously downloaded books were lifesavers. There is no feeling for a book lover like having 4 or 5 books at one's disposal, being able to switch between books at one's own convenience, and escaping the isolation of traveling long hours on an airplane.

However, when it comes time to download a new book, or dictionary in my case, what does one do? If you are stuck with a long layover in the Narita Airport in Tokyo, Japan, downloading a new book is not as easy as simply switching on the Kindle's wireless and browsing the online bookstore.

Amazon's Whispernet wireless technology, available anywhere in the United States, is not accessible outside of the US. For this reason Kindle users must rely on other wireless Internet access sources while traveling. Since Narita International Airport claims to have easy wireless Internet access, I had thought my Kindle would continue to be useful before even arriving at my destination. However, connecting to wireless in airports is rarely as easy as simply turning your wireless on. A computer can open multiple windows and simplifies the connection process. Then you can usually download wirelessly to the computer. The Kindle, on the other hand, cannot open multiple windows, so trying to sign on to the Narita Wireless via Kindle's Internet was futile.

While repeatedly trying to sign on to the Narita system, the Kindle's Internet (which was in its "experimental" phase in January) continually crashed and froze my Kindle. Restarting a Kindle can be nerve racking the 5th time around, especially when you know that almost a month's worth of your reading and research materials are available only on it! Narita: 1. Kindle: 0.

In general, downloading books to one's computer via wireless is easy, as is transferring those downloads to the Kindle. However, travelers be warned: travel with the appropriate cords at all times in the event that the Kindle cannot connect to a wireless source, and thus cannot download purchased books. In this case, you must download to your computer, and then connect to your Kindle by USB. This is hardly the ideal set-up.

My traveling companions, one of whom owned a Kindle, one who had an iPad, and one who had recently purchased the Barnes and Noble Color Nook, rarely faced the same problems as I. They had either downloaded enough books prior to their trip or, in the case of the Nook holder, had no problems downloading via wireless access that required multiple internet windows to connect.

Another problem I faced when trying to download books in China in particular was getting books that may be banned in that country. I had thought that simply copying materials that I needed to read for my studies to a word document and then transferring the word document to my Kindle via my computer would easily amend this problem.

However, Microsoft Word documents often crash the Kindle, most notably when there were tables or complicated charts that need to be viewed more clearly. PDFs do not do much better, but very simple word documents pose no difficulty for a Kindle reader.

Were Amazon able to fix the glitches in the Kindle web browser so that Internet access was possible in areas where there is an Internet key required, my Kindle would have been far more useful. The bottom line: Kindle users must be prepared if they are traveling to Asia—have your books downloaded beforehand and bring all your computer and Kindle cords with you so that transferring documents will be more accessible.

Also, if you are traveling with a Nook or iPad user, make sure that you have some truly interesting reads—the lack of entertainment provided on a Kindle, outside of your books or magazines, can be magnified when surrounded by those with media devices that provide more visual interaction, such as our group's main entertainment, "Angry Birds."

A Kindle add-on that I highly recommend is the Kindle Lighted Leather Cover (http://amzn.to/lI0MeU). This provides a great light that is a savior on dark buses or when sharing a hotel room with a traveling companion. In fact, my one complaint would be that the light is almost too bright, but does serve as a nice flashlight when needed.

So, Kindle users who travel abroad: plan your trips accordingly. A Kindle can be a wonderful companion, but without the right preparation, can cause many frustrations. Oh, and don't forget: all electronics must be shut off before takeoff.

Overlays and the Optimal User Experience

Michael Geraci
Associate Professor of Media Arts, Pacific University

The concept of *flow* as a human condition is attributed to Hungarian psychologist Mihaly Csikszentmihalyi [1] whose book, *Flow: The Psychology of Optimal Experience* (1990) is considered the primary text in this field of research. At one time or another, most of us have experienced flow – a state of such focused concentration and absorption that our minds are virtually free of our bodies and we lose track of all worldly concerns such as time, hunger, and physical comfort. Athletes, artists, writers, and even software programmers often refer to such experiences when they are fully engaged in their craft and operating at the peak of their abilities.

If we generalize and simplify just a bit from Csikszentmihalyi's notion of pure flow, it is reasonable to say that there is a certain level of flow that is possible in our daily interactions with popular media. It is commonplace to "lose oneself" in a great book, or to be nonplussed at the realization that one has played a highly immersive video game through the night and into morning. The cinema itself, with its massive screen, darkened interior and enveloping sound system is designed to transport us into the fantastic world projected before us, allowing us to forget where we are if only for an hour or two.

So what about the Web? How much flow have we come to expect from this burgeoning medium? Do we, as users, sit down at our computers and prepare to lose ourselves in the world of information that awaits us? This is not so difficult to imagine when the Web is replicating traditional mediated experiences, such as playing full-screen video or interactive content, it begins to feel a bit flow-like, but I would argue that it is in the replication of these more common experiences (watching TV, playing games, etc.) that flow is more attainable since our minds are somewhat predisposed to engaging in such content via their traditional means of delivery. However, when it comes to information retrieval, decision-making, knowledge building and discourse on the Web, we've never really expected that the notion of flow was even possible.

Kevin Kelly, author of the *Whole Earth Review* and Executive Editor at *Wired* said, "It's really amazing that all this stuff [on the Web] is here. It's in 5,000 days, all this stuff has come. And I know that 10 years ago, if I had told you that this

---

[1] http://www.ted.com/talks/lang/eng/mihaly_csikszentmihalyi_on_flow.html

was all coming, you would have said that 'that's impossible'." [2] And he's right, of course. We had no idea the Web would be the way it is today when we first began to imagine what would happen ten years later.

It is in this context and with a bit of hope and optimism that I feel that the Web will attain the capacity for flow. To be clear, I'm not talking about losing track of time while surfing the Web. My adapted version of Csikszentmihalyi's flow is simply to say that there can and should be unhindered and uninterrupted immersion in the stream of information we are able to receive and act upon. A stream that knows enough about us and the nature of our information needs to react in real-time and always be presenting us with the next logical step in our journey. Free of bounces back and forth between search results and disconnected pages; and devoid of the inevitable "log-in to see this" dialogues, this new vision of the Web is more like a seemingly endless conversation with an expert; a two-way dialogue that builds in complexity and scope as it progresses. It will change our models for education, e-commerce, and development within our professions.

My belief that this is entirely possible within the next iteration of the Web (maybe it will be the defining characteristic of "Web 3.0") is based upon certain indicators that are quickly becoming the standard design patterns* of the modern Web coupled with the natural inclination for all media to evolve to modes of more immersive experiences (witness the 3D television hype circa 2010).

One of the primary indicators of a move towards keeping users in the flow is the move away from pop-up windows to in-context overlays. Overlays, according to Bill Scott [3] and Theresa Neil [4] in *Designing Web Interfaces* [5] are objects that are lightweight, unobtrusive, fast to load, and visually integrated into the design of a site, which are useful for gathering user input, displaying more information, providing instruction, or asking questions. You've probably become familiar with overlays if you browse online photo galleries, use NetFlix.com regularly, or "look inside" books at Amazon . com. An overlay opens up a floating information object that allows you to interact with information directly or browse through a related or more specific set of information without having to leave the current page and therefore not having to wait through page reloads and "hub and spoke" navigational models (Figure 1).

---

[2] http://www.ted.com/talks/lang/eng/kevin_kelly_on_the_next_5_000_days_of_the_web.html

[3] http://looksgoodworkswell.blogspot.com/

[4] http://www.designgenie.org/

[5] http://designingwebinterfaces.com/

Figure 1 Lightbox in action

The free Lightbox [6] library of JavaScripts for displaying photo or video media in a darkened pane above your current Web page has been around for a number of years and has become the standard for presenting images (and, more currently, videos or interactive modules), but e-commerce powerhouses know that flow heightens the browsing experience, which in turn leads to sales. Netflix.com keeps you looking at as many film titles as possible while calling up a personalized overlay with each mouse hover over a film graphic. The quick overlay has all the information one would need to make an informed decision about whether or not to select a film for viewing (Figure 2) and the browsing application progresses to a much more functional overlay once a title is actually selected for the queue. This secondary overlay (again delivered right on top of the current page) lets you promote your recent selection to the top of your viewing list and presents you with ten other titles you might want to act upon based on your last selection. From a purely economic point of view, Netflix wants its users to fill their queues with as many enjoyable films as possible and their well-designed overlay system combined with their suggestion algorithm makes a strong case for renewing that monthly subscription again and again.

---

[6] http://www.lokeshdhakar.com/projects/lightbox2/

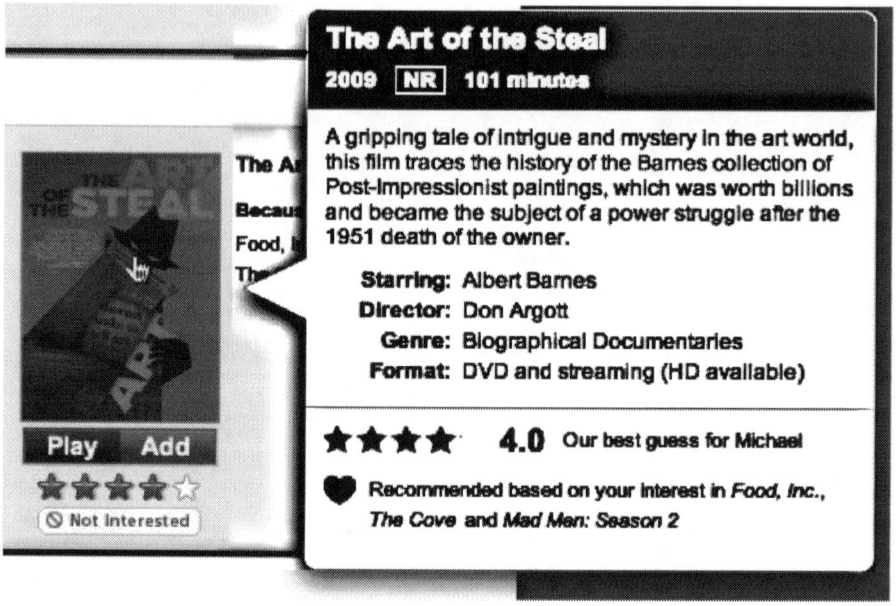

Figure 2 A quick hover-triggered overlay on Netflix.com

Amazon, no slouch in the online retailing universe, also uses customized and full-featured overlays in their bookstore. They know all too well that people *like* browsing the shelves of brick and mortar stores. One find leads to another, one concept or author opens up a world of possibilities. Amazon's look inside feature gives you more information about a book by letting you flip through it, browse and even search its contents (is my Kindle full yet?). Like Netflix, the user is presented with personalized options for more books related to the current one and one's own buying history.

The beauty of the overlay is that it is easily dismissed (click anywhere outside the overlay's content) and it furthers the experience. It is one step closer to flow in the browsing experience. On Amazon, it's as close as one gets to flipping through the book in your right hand while keeping your place inside the book in your left hand with your finger.

Overlays are the harbingers of what is to come. Better browsers, quicker code execution, and the semantic** Web will embed a steady flow of relevant information into our browsing experiences, while background intelligence connects us to concepts and information products that will keep our minds occupied and our imaginations afire with an endless conversation with an expert.

Notes

* "Design pattern" is a term coined by Christopher Alexander in *A Pattern Language: Towns, Buildings, Construction* (1977) that refers to "...a problem which occurs over and over again in our environment, and then describes the core solution to that problem." This concept was adapted to engineering, programming and information architecture. Put simply, design patterns are a model for capturing, organizing, and building a shared vocabulary of best practices.

** The semantic Web is considered to be the next stage in the evolution of the Web. It involves an underlying intelligence on the Web that automatically understands the context of information and builds logical connections between current and related content. Imagine automatically generated hyperlinks!

Editor's Note

Interface published an article dealing with the concept of flow and game addiction by Alexander E. Voiskounsky of the Psychology Department, Moscow Lomonosov State. Please see it at:
http://bcis.pacificu.edu/journal/2007/06/voiskounsky.php

A Review of the iPad After One Year

Greg Orlowsky & Peter Orlowsky

Editor's Note:

Greg is a highly valued member of the Instructional Technology team at Pacific University, widely know as the "Apple Guy," who solves many of our tech issues and invariably gives good advice to the Berglund Center. Peter is his son, a highly wired high school student.

Usability by Peter:

My backpack used to weigh upwards of 35 pounds. It was so cluttered with notebooks, binders, and textbooks that it was literally weighing me down. What is funny is that I barely noticed this weighty disorganization. I had learned to adapt and work with it, at least until I got my iPad.

The world shook when the iPad was released; Steve Jobs ushered it into mainstream consciousness as "A revolutionary product." Through this clamor and buzz
we were told that the iPad would be a monumental educational product. They were right.

While the thousands of apps available to consumers center mostly around wasting time and providing a distraction (Angry birds) I have found that if you try hard enough you can actually transform the iPad into a tool for almost all aspects of education. I firmly believe that it has made me into a better student. What most don't realize, however, is that the iPad doesn't come this way; it is simply a shell for the 300,000+ apps available to it.

When I first bought my iPad it came with virtually nothing installed (what a great pun). All I had to go off of was a calendar, a rudimentary note taker, a connection to the Internet, and the App store. What makes the iPad so unique and allows for such a strong human connection is that as you learn, it adapts.

I remember the first day I brought it to class; after pulling it out in first period English and getting all the "ooh's" and "ahh's" from my fellow students out of the way, the teacher began handing out essay prompts for us to begin drafting. That essay took me all of fifteen minutes to write, edit, and email directly to my teacher. I used Pages for iPad, which I downloaded using my school's Wi-Fi, and spent fifteen minutes on a project I would have otherwise done overnight. As school days dragged on I began to develop a collection of apps that suited all my classes' needs. Now about the only things in my backpack are my iPad and a solitary folder of worksheets.

Essential Education Apps

iWork for iPad: allows you to share documents, create Power Points, and build spreadsheets — a must have.

Graph Calculator HD: solve those pesky math problems with this full function graphing calculator.

Sound Note: record what your teacher says in the form of an audio recording, as well as a written document.

iStudiez Pro: the student planner of your dreams— never miss an assignment again.

Support by Greg:

I will now discuss supporting the iPad over the last year. All I can say is that it is a rock solid device. We have had no system crashes and only one app crash. The only errors we have experienced have been self-induced—like when I updated the OS without saving my documents. It is important to update documents daily with Dropbox or some other cloud storage. Using iTunes is a little cumbersome. By the way, it has been months since we have attached the iPad to a computer. It just doesn't need to be connected that much.

We deployed a few iPads to the Early Learning Center in the College of Education at Pacific. I expected calls for Wi-Fi problems or lost files, but that has not occurred. I was in class the other day supporting a MacBook that was having issues with Wi-Fi; the kids at the next table were oblivious to my problems because their iPad was working flawlessly. It was Dr. Seuss day after all. The lack of support required for this device is a real money saver. It makes it easy to justify to your CIO when he does not have to budget for much support for the device.

One question still remains: can an iPad be a stand-alone device? The answer, in my opinion, is both yes and no. If you are tied heavily to the cloud, I believe it could be your only device. A real bonus is support for Bluetooth keyboards. Support for more accessories is in the pipeline. If, however, you are a video producer or need a lot of processor power, you may need a more powerful machine. By the way, iPad rocks for audio creation. It is the marriage of hardware and software to advance learning and growth that makes the iPad the game changer that it is.

Update: iPad 2

A few days ago (March 11, 2011) iPad2 was released. I wanted to include my thoughts on this updated hardware. As is usually the case, Apple again has done its homework and gave us the features that were missing on the 1.0 release. Apple is famous for what is intentionally left out. Again, no support for Flash (I consider that a plus by the way). The camera is the prime upgrade this time. It is nothing to write home about, but it is there. The placement of the lens is a little awkward. My finger covered it several times. FaceTime really works well though. The large screen gives it enough real estate to make the experience more intimate.

Another major difference is the slimness and weight loss. It lost 33% of its height and now has curved edges. It is a delight to hold compared to the original, and losing the .2 lbs. makes it feel much lighter in the hand.

iPad 2 boasts a much better processor, now a dual core A5 chip. It also sports up to 9X better graphics performance. The gamers will love this addition and the opportunities for augmented reality apps will be huge for developers.

Lastly, the iOS 4.3 update adds full screen support for projecting the whole screen to a TV or projector. This will be beneficial for smart classrooms. An HDMI adapter is also available, great for viewing on a big screen TV. There is also better Home Network sharing with iOS 4.3. It is great not to have to load Movies on the iPad when you can stream from your computer.

In a few weeks the original iPad inventory will dry up, but you will not lose anything as the iPad 2 is a better machine. I do not feel slighted though as an owner of the original iPad. iOS 4.3 has a few goodies that keep the original iPad an evolving, improving platform.

Book Reviews – Volume 11

Jeffrey Barlow – *Dan Breznitz and Michael Murphree, Run of the Red Queen*
http://bcis.pacificu.edu/interface/?p=645

Jeffrey Barlow – *Daniel Henrich's Internet Evangelism in the 21st Century*
http://bcis.pacificu.edu/interface/?p=279

Jeffrey Barlow – *Detective/Mystery Fiction and the Impact of the Internet: The Edgar Nominees for 2011*
http://bcis.pacificu.edu/interface/?p=361

Jeffrey Barlow – *Edgar Award Nominees, 2011, and the Impact of the Internet, Part II*
http://bcis.pacificu.edu/interface/?p=426

Richard Tinsen & Mike Charles – *Jason Ohler's Digital Community: Digital Citizen*
http://bcis.pacificu.edu/interface/?p=285

Jeffrey Barlow – *Robert Glenn Howard's Digital Jesus*
http://bcis.pacificu.edu/interface/?p=494

Jeffrey Barlow – *Tim Elmore's Generation iY: Our Last Chance to Save Their Future*
http://bcis.pacificu.edu/interface/?p=503

Dan Breznitz and Michael Murphree, *Run of the Red Queen*

Government, Innovation, Globalization and Economic Growth in China. New Haven: Yale University Press, 2011

Review by Jeffrey Barlow

At the Berglund Center we have long been interested in the relationship between the impact of the Internet and economic development. [1] While there is no doubt that there is a relationship between these two factors, its precise nature is difficult to quantify.

Some argue, for example, that economic development is largely a unified process regardless of time or location, and that positive changes in productivity, investment, and other econometric factors will inevitably facilitate development. [2] Others believe, however, that local culture remains the critical factor in development and that if there is a mismatch between culture and informational technology (IT), development will not necessarily occur regardless of econometric improvements. [3]

One of the important questions in understanding contemporary political and economic development is the extent to which the Chinese model provides a useful example for other emerging economies, or perhaps even for highly developed ones. The question of particularistic cultural issues vs. a universal process is especially salient as cultural differences are inherent to such comparisons.

Some argue that China's development is inherently limited because it does not follow the Western model. China can take advantage of low cost labor, manipulate its currency, and otherwise scramble up the ladder of development. But the ultimate success of any model depends in this formulation on its ability to innovate. [4] Lacking the ability to lead in innovative technology, Chinese success will remain simply duplicative; it copies others and fundamentally relies

---

[1] Among our reviews and discussions of this issue in Interface see: Berger, Suzanne and Richard K. Lester (eds.) Global Taiwan: Building Competitive Strengths in a New International Economy. New York: M.E. Sharpe, 2005. http://bcis.pacificu.edu/journal/article.php?id=233

[2] For this perspective see: Robert D and Andrew S. McKay. Digital Prosperity: Understanding the Economic Benefits of the Information Technology Revolution. The Information Technology & Innovation Foundation. http://bcis.pacificu.edu/journal/article.php?id=201

[3] See: Kenny, Charles. Overselling the Web? Development and the Internet. London: Lynne Rienner Publishers at: http://bcis.pacificu.edu/journal/article.php?id=201 and Payal Arora. Dot Com Mantra. Social Computing in the Central Himalayas. http://bcis.pacificu.edu/journal/article.php?id=739.

[4] Breznitz and Murphree, 2.

upon temporary advantages presented by its particular mix of labor and other resources. These facts being, true, then, China will never reach the top rung. In short, because of its failure to foster innovation, other economies have little to learn from it.

Breznitz and Murphree take quite a different perspective. Both are academics at the Sam Nunn School of International Affairs at the Georgia Institute of Technology. Breznitz is the author of a significant previous work, *Innovation and the State.* [5] The two argue that the global reorganization of production and services consequent to the development of the Internet and digital communications has given rise to new means of creating value, and that China excels in these.

The two believe that in the post-Internet era, innovation per se is much less important than it once was, and chain production processes make the Chinese economy fully sustainable in both the immediate and long run. China in essence quickly capitalizes upon the technological advances of others and maintains its productive forces just behind the cutting edge of technology. Hence the metaphor, the "Run of the Red Queen," a term for an economy which must, like the Queen in *Alice in Wonderland*, run as fast as she can just to keep up.

One of China's strengths in this particular process is the presence of a number of distinctive economic regions, each with varying economic policies and resources, which are deployed in an unending quest for local advantages. Some particular industries or production processes will fail to develop in some localities, but profiting from a different mix of policies and resources will succeed in others.

Neither is this model dependent upon the development of entire industries as such, but often succeeds by occupying a niche in a widely distributed production chain. China does not need to produce automobiles, for example, but simply to become the most efficient producer in supplying particular parts and processes contributing to the final product.

Moreover, from a theoretical perspective, this approach is quite different from previous models such as that of Taiwan, Korea or Singapore, often termed the "fast follower model." China brings to bear additional advantages such as a rapidly developing local consumer market, a very successful export process and quick access to foreign investment capital, as well as access to new technologies.

As the authors point out, there are important elements of paradox in this Chinese success story. The national government, for example, continues to

---

[5] See citations and references at: http://scholar.google.com/scholar?q=breznitz+innovation+state&hl=en&as_sdt=0&as_vis=1&oi=scholart

emphasize in its policies the importance of research and innovation. But it is in the local areas that the model has proven successful.

The central approach of the authors is to study three different regions and their IT industries. These are Beijing, Shanghai, and the Pearl River Delta centered upon Shenzhen. The authors argue that "these regional systems combine to form a unique, de facto *national* innovation system and that without understanding this system and how it interacts with the regional system, we will fail to understand China." [6]

The authors' careful analysis of each region, supported by both a sound understanding of previous research and by many interviews with critical actors, is persuasive. In the case of the IT firms of Beijing, for example, the central problem is the lack of capital investment for start-ups. The central government privileges well established and particularly state-owned firms, and hence central banking policies tend to allocate capital to such firms. But the Beijing municipality or local government has created a number of devices for easing the access to developmental capital to local start-ups, many of which have proven successful. [7]

Shanghai, unlike Beijing, has a plentiful supply of cheap labor. [8] Its local government accordingly privileges foreign investment (Taiwanese investment would be included here), which takes advantage of that cheap labor for production. The Shanghai government offers a rich mix of financial and organizational incentives to attract both foreign R&D and capital. This gives Shanghai a distinctive profile of being directly influenced and guided by local policy and central planning which tends to favor state-owned and well-established firms, unlike Beijing. These firms are, however, like Shanghai itself, conspicuously successful.

The Shanghai model, while quite different from that of Beijing, is highly complementary. It would not be unusual, for example, for a firm to begin in Beijing with its foundation in the highly developed local educational institutions with their rich intellectual resources, then outsource actual manufacturing to Shanghai with its strong support for such industries.

The Pearl River Delta (Shenzhen principally) is often thought of both in China and abroad, as China's sweatshop. However, it also hosts several of leading Chinese IT innovators, including Huawei, ZTE and Tencent (QQ). [9] The PRD firms do prize innovation, but in a very incremental and measured fashion which

---

[6] 8.
[7] 119-125.
[8] For Shanghai analysis see Chapter 4.
[9] For the PRD see Chapter 5.

might well be taken to be beneath the threshold of the usual meaning of the term.

Nonetheless, this careful process has developed a number of significant firms, which effectively integrate all stages of the production process from R&D through to final export. Because it is the individual firms that undertake these initiatives, the IT industry of the Pearl River Delta is collectively very nimble and market oriented. It tends to be both isolated from political power and focused equally on domestic and foreign markets.

This Chinese system, as successful as it is—it has, after all, contributed to the longest and most successful run of economic development of any human society—is not without its hazards. The central government can often be a negative factor as it responds to political or economic pressures or attempts to model upon inappropriate foreign models, as in its ongoing attempt to produce a Chinese equivalent of Microsoft or Silicon Valley. [10]

The work is primarily intended for an academic audience, but it has found a much wider readership (it has been very well reviewed in the business periodical press) in large part because, although sometimes fairly technical, it is written in a clear prose with a minimum of econometric data. The notes and references are voluminous, permitting the reader to access markedly different perspectives or better understand the literature, which has contributed to the authors' conclusions.

Run of the Red Queen makes, we think, many important contributions to furthering our understanding of IT and the impact of the Internet, our understanding of economic development, and our understanding of China. It should be read by anybody wishing to better understand these topics.

---

[10] For shortcomings of the model see 197-98.

Daniel Henrich's Internet Evangelism in the 21st Century

Jeffrey Barlow
An Editorial Review

This is a relatively old book intended to introduce highly evangelical Christians to the use of the web as a tool for proselytism. We review it less as a book to be read by others, though it may indeed be useful to some, than for what it tells us about religion on the web.

Religion and the WWW is not a new topic for us. [1] One of our most popular book reviews---as indicated by the fact that the traffic crashed our server when it was "digged" shortly after we posted it--- was Peter D. Hershock's work, *Reinventing the Wheel: A Buddhist Response to the Information Age.* [2]

We cannot recommend this book for a wide audience simply because it is deliberately intended for a rather narrow one: Christian evangelicals who wish to learn to use the web to proselytize. The book came out of a 2005 conference, "Internet Evangelism for the 21st Century" at Liberty University in Lynchburg, Virginia on web evangelism. The book incorporates, fairly directly, the transcripts of 21 workshops held at the conference and presented by well-known Internet evangels.

The book is edited by Henrich, though it might be considered to have been written by him more than edited; he is clearly the guiding light among the Internet evangels. He has a great deal of experience as a consultant as well as a practitioner, apparently largely within college environments.

The audience for the conference was primarily evangelical Christians, whom many might consider to be among the most conservative of Americans. The blend of traditional protestant religious approaches and references to the WWW is very interesting. The book is a fascinating one because it is evident that this conference indicated a sort of turning point for many evangelicals, perhaps the first time they were exposed to practitioners who had successfully used the Web. As the transcripts show, many participants had a certain amount of resistance to the idea of electronic evangelism. Evangelism, especially in these particular

---

[1] Fair disclosure: If asked (usually while teaching in China) what my religious beliefs might be, I reply that I am a Christian or a Buddhist on alternate days. I have occasionally subbed for the ministers in my local United Methodist church and attended Buddhist rites in China, Taiwan, Japan, and Vietnam as well as in the U.S.

[2] See the latter half of a review article which leads off with a work irrelevant to this discussion at: http://bcis.pacificu.edu/journal/article.php?id=185

churches, has long been extremely personal and very face-to-face in its approach[3]. Growing up in Southern Illinois, in a largely rural area, I was exposed to many touring tent evangels and always found, regardless of how I felt about any particular theological message, that the preachers had a very sharp understanding of their audience which depended on their ability to quickly "read" participants in a brief personal meeting.

The big tent message seemed to me to serve primarily to permit the preachers to identify audience members who might be further cultivated, for religious purposes, of course. It would have been impossible for me to imagine at the time that anything resembling the World Wide Web might one day be viewed by such preachers as a useful tool.

The churches at that time (1950's) tended not to make a very good use of even film. Touring religious films were not unusual, but often had very low production values featuring biblical spectaculars, such as the flood, the mass drowning of pursuing Egyptians, or the destruction of Sodom. The newspapers ads, as often as not, featured Eve en route to the The Fall, her offending bits artfully concealed by fig leaves, apples, or a serpent.

These films were what Hollywood disparagingly called, "Four Wallers for the Goon Trade," meaning films which were distributed through an area almost simultaneously and for which tickets were often sold to church groups.[4] A recent much more sophisticated---and highly successful--- example of a religious film, of course, was Mel Gibson's "The Passion of the Christ. [5]

The primary media tool of evangelicals in the U.S. was first the radio, at which many were adept. A common approach was to blend American folk music, not always of the religious sort, with their messages. Later, of course, evangelicals took with equal success and fervor to Television.

---

[3] For a useful discussion of McLuhan's distinction pertinent to this piece, see *Bob's Blog* at http://bobington.blogspot.com/2007/02/hot-and-cold-media.html
[4] In 1979 a very successful film, "The Jesus Film," was very effectively used, particularly in evangelizing abroad. Some credit this single film for most of the conversions made in the developing world since that date. See the project site at: http://www.jesusfilm.org/
[5] There is a very thorough Wikipedia article on this film found at: http://en.wikipedia.org/wiki/The_Passion_of_the_Christ As it is largely about the making of the film and the controversies around it, it may be of limited utility for many readers. We have to hope that such details as the statement that the assistant director was twice struck by lightning while filming in Italy are both true and irrelevant in a theological sense.

When compared to either radio or television, however, the Internet seems a much "colder" medium.[6] Too, as the Internet has developed, it has come with a great deal of baggage, including pornography and other content which the fundamentalist Christians view as extremely degraded and sinful. The impact of such content on Christian youth is a particular concern, of course.

For evangelicals to even consider going onto the WWW then, is a really remarkable development which runs counter to their traditions of face-to-face proselytizing as well as requiring the use of what is sometimes thought of as Satan's sharpest new tool.[7]

As the book makes clear, however, the evangelical churches, like the older "mainline" denominations were, at the time of the conference in 1995, suffering substantial losses in memberships. This was particularly true among younger Christians, and overall the number of un-churched Americans was growing very rapidly.

This problem was most usually presented in the work as a sort of cultural gap; the Boomer generation making up most congregations were beginning to encounter Gen-X youth who were much less interested in formal church membership than they were interested in the Internet.

It seems from the presenters at the conference that the use of the Internet for evangelizing began on college campuses, particularly with the Campus Crusade for Christ. It has frequently been the case in American history that progressive religious movements have begun on campuses. These college congregations produced a number of electronic evangels, who then worked into more established organizations, such as the Billy Graham Crusade, from which several of the presenters also came.

On balance, the book represents many of the most notable practitioners of digital evangelism and serves as a very useful introduction to the important issues facing them. Again we can see the widespread impact of the Internet on a niche audience.

---

[6] For a useful discussion of McLuhan's distinction between hot and cold media pertinent to this piece, see *Bob's Blog* at http://bobington.blogspot.com/2007/02/hot-and-cold-media.html
[7] See a discussion to this point on "My Digital Life" at: http://www.mydigitallife.co.za/index.php?option=com_myblog&show=2331&Itemid=29. Clearly this is sometimes tongue in cheek though the original posting seems sincere.

Many of the conference panels were addressed to very basic issues such as how to optimize page views, effectively use Google key words, developing podcasts ("Godcasts"), religiously themed blogs, chat rooms and other media formats. The speakers are, in some cases, confrontational with the local audience as they try to overcome established evangelical opinions, which they frankly challenge as prejudicial ones.

There is certainly a pronounced preacherly or evangelical style to the discussions. A common opening to the pieces, which are as much transcripts of an oral event as prepared papers, is a confessional one. Here the presenter offers up his or her past evil behavior, relates seemingly miraculous cures, and other tropes of American evangelical Protestantism. There are very few female voices, and seemingly no Catholic ones. But among the group are very sophisticated techies, some of whom are quite familiar with very advanced forms of digital communications, and all of whom are highly committed both to their digital congregations and to their shared religious views.

Who should read this book? Anyone interested in maximizing their electronic audiences for their web pages or other digital media would find many of the examples utilized here very useful, though there may be many culturally more comfortable ways of securing the same information on the web or through mainstream publications. Other audiences may find the tone and content of the book off-putting. But it is fascinating to see the impact of the Web upon that old time religion, and eye opening to see the great technical sophistication as well as the high level of tolerance of these electronic evangelicals.

Detective/Mystery Fiction and the Impact of the Internet: The Edgar Nominees for 2011

Jeffrey Barlow

Edgar Award Nominees, 2011, and the Impact of the Internet

Harlan Coben's, Caught (Dutton Adult, 2010)

David Gordon's The Serialist: A Novel (Simon & Schuster, 2010)

This is another installment in an *Interface* series weighing the impact of the Internet by analyzing award winning detective or mystery fiction. [1] The works we examine are selected from the nominees of the most highly regarded of U.S. awards in this category, the annual Edgar Allan Poe awards presented by the Mystery Writers of America. [2] The Edgar nominees for 2011 (for books published in 2010) were announced on January 19th 2011 on the 202nd birthday of Edgar Allan Poe. The winners will be announced in New York on April 28, 2011. [3]

Our methodology is a very simple one. We are interested almost solely in how the award-winning authors incorporate (or inappropriately ignore) the Internet

---

[1] For previous pieces in the series see: Forward to a New Article Series: Detective Fiction and the Internet: http://bcis.pacificu.edu/journal/article.php?id=691 See also the review of C.J. Box, Blue Heaven, found at: http://bcis.pacificu.edu/journal/article.php?id=698 and the review of John Hart's work, The Last Child at: http://bcis.pacificu.edu/journal/article. php?id=728

[2] For the current Edgar awards site, go to: http://www.theedgars.com/nominees.html

[3] The nominees are: **Best novel**

- *Caught* by Harlan Coben (Penguin Group USA - Dutton)
- *Crooked Letter, Crooked Letter* by Tom Franklin (HarperCollins - William Morrow)
- *Faithful Place* by Tana French (Penguin Group USA - Viking)
- *The Queen of Patpong* by Timothy Hallinan (HarperCollins - William Morrow)
- *The Lock Artist* by Steve Hamilton (Minotaur/Thomas Dunne Books)
- *I'd Know You Anywhere* by Laura Lippman (HarperCollins - William Morrow)

Best first novels

- *Rogue Island* by Bruce DeSilva (Tom Doherty Associates - Forge Books)
- *The Poacher's Son* by Paul Doiron (Minotaur Books)
- *The Serialist*: A Novel by David Gordon (Simon & Schuster)
- *Galveston* by Nic Pizzolatto (Simon & Schuster - Scribner)
- *Snow Angels* by James Thompson (Penguin Group USA - G.P. Putnam's Sons)

in constructing their plots. This is a particularly useful approach for evaluating the impact of the Internet because, by its nature, the genre of mystery or detective fiction is most often focused on missing information. Usually that information is the identity of the perpetrator or criminal. The slang title for these works, "whodunit," is particularly appropriate.

The classical works in the genre have almost invariably begun with a crime, and then set a sleuth to solve that crime by parsing the known information to arrive at the solution. Authors have gone to incredible lengths to complicate the puzzle thus set for the sleuth and for the reader. Such complications have often reached kabuki-like stylizations. For example, the old "locked room" subset of the genre presents a scene within which the crime—usually murder— seems to be impossible. The crime scene was locked or otherwise isolated, no weapon is found, the cause of death is unclear, and any number of other tropes is introduced. Works range from Poe's own 1841 piece, *The Murders in the Rue Morgue* (often said to be the earliest fully developed example of the type), to many foreign language examples. [4] However, despite their occasional uses, such stylized scenarios as the locked room or the isolated island no longer seem realistic to contemporary readers.

The advent of the Internet has complicated mystery plotting because so much more information is available to both the sleuth and the reader. The reader is not likely to remain long interested in a detective who is too dumb to take the obvious first step in any research—going on line for related information.

There are a number of ways to avoid this problem. Some stories do not, of course, require outright evasion because of the setting; often the story develops in the past. Authors have many legitimate reasons for ignoring technology. A recent nominee for the Edgar Award for 2010 in the category Best Critical / Biographical Work , P.D. James' *Talking About Detective Fiction*, discussed one such reason. For James, the classical pre-war and post-war mystery authors, such as Agatha Christie, wrote in the golden age of detective fiction. They set their stories in a much less troubled past, often in an almost timeless village, precisely because they wanted their readers to escape from the real world. In those setting the universe of information was very circumscribed and plots often depended upon character development.

The current time period seems to us to be one of transition. The Internet or digital communications are omnipresent now. But authors are still not entirely

---

[4] There is a very thorough analysis of this sub-genre to be found at: http://en.wikipedia.org/wiki/ Locked_room_mystery. Sadly, it lacks adequate citations, but it is a good place to understand the development of the genre, if not a good guide to the important sources.

comfortable with it. Reactions range from authors who all but ignore the Internet, to those who are learning to make good use of it in their stories.

However, ignoring the Internet now is not easy. In analyzing Edgar winners for 2009 and 2010, we made this observation:

> *"The Internet is unavoidable in even relatively isolated plot settings provided that the time period includes it. But plotting often demands that it be carefully restricted in its use until crucial moments. The trope then, requires some explanation for the failure to employ the Internet until the necessary moment."* [5]

In our opinion the Edgar winners for Best Novels in 2009 or 2010 failed to deal adequately with the impact of the Internet. In that sense, the genre is potentially in trouble. Audiences must not feel deliberately misled, nor should questions as to the wisdom of the sleuth arise in their minds. Newer and younger audiences in particular want some sense of cultural relevance in their readings.

This year we are reading all the works that are not set in a time before the Internet which have been nominated either for Best Novel, or for Best First Novel. We choose both categories on the assumption that the authors in the latter may be younger, and possibly more comfortable with the Internet. Dame James, a winner of the Mystery Writers of America Grand Master title in 1999 and author of the superb British series featuring Inspector Adam Dalgliesh, as well as many other works,, had something to say about computers and age groups. After describing the evolution of the technology with which she has written over thirty years, she wrote: "Finally it (a manuscript) is sent simultaneously to my publisher, agent, and editor through cyberspace, a system which I can neither operate nor understand." [6] This unfamiliarity with the Internet is not a problem for Dame James, because most of her works are set before its advent.

---

[5] To see my full analysis of this conclusion go to: http://bcis.pacificu.edu/journal/article.php?id=698

[6] P.D. James, *Talking about Detective Fiction*, Kindle Edition, loc 1608-10.

In discussing e-readers, after expressing her commitment to conventional books, she writes:

> *"What is surprising is not that the detective story has altered, but that it has survived, and that what we have seen since the interwar years has been development, not a rejection, followed by renewal."* [7]

We too are pleased that the genre is undergoing a renewal. Below we review two Edgar nominees for 2011, to see what more may be learned about the impact of the Internet on the genre.

Warning: Plot Spoilers Below...

To begin, we selected from among the nominees Harlan Coben's work, Caught. Coben will be a familiar name to most who read in mystery or detective fiction. [8] He is not only a prolific best-selling author, but also a critically acclaimed one who has already won one Edgar and been nominated for two others. He has also won several major British awards as well as the French *Le Grand Prix des Lectrices de Elle* for fiction. On the basis of success and reputation, many might consider Coben to be the favorite in this year's Edgar competition.

Caught is also very useful in our attempt to analyze the use of the Internet in mystery fiction. It would be difficult to contrive a more Internet-centered plot. It is, however, a very convoluted plot and certainly not easy to summarize.

The protagonist, "Wendy," is a TV personality who has exposed "Dan" on the air. He is accused of stalking a teen-ager on the Internet. Wendy's program was built around a sting intended to brand him as just that: a stalker of young girls. However, her exposure of him leads to his murder by a vengeful relative of a missing girl. Wendy, however, begins to trust her reportorial instincts more than the circumstantial evidence she has followed which had apparently gotten Dan killed.

Coben presents the Internet in a very realistic fashion. It becomes a major factor in both the crimes and in their solutions. Wendy is a facile and experienced Internet researcher. She moves from simple uses of the Internet to accessing large databases and then on to Facebook, which turns out to be a critical source of evidence. For an audience with some experience with similar social sites, her path seems both logical and self-affirming. This is the way we would do it too.

---

[7] P.D. James, *Talking about Detective Fiction*, Kindle Edition, loc 1612 and following.

[8] See the author's page at: http://www.harlancoben.com/static/bio.htm

But Wendy's search begins to suggest that Dan was the victim of a very sophisticated smear artist who had used email and the Internet to entangle him in her sting. From there, she herself becomes a victim, as the possible perpetrator (who is perhaps involved in the abduction and murder of the missing young women himself) smears her on the Internet as a harassing seductress who will stop at nothing in building her career. She is fired. This then requires that she become personally involved in an informal search to solve the crime, although with great help from a bevy of friends and contacts.

Caught was successful throughout in incorporating new media, the Internet, pop culture (such as music), a poor economy, dying newspapers, and all the tropes of our present digital world. Wendy seems an appropriate hero for the present who employs the tools of her profession in solving crime, much as Sherlock Holmes employed his own scientific knowledge.

We have no clue, of course, as to whether or not *Caught* will win the Edgar for Best First Novel this year. But so far as making good use of the Internet and constructing a plot around such timely issues as identity theft and online bullying, not to mention Coben's previous career, the work is certainly a major contender.

Because we want to see if younger authors are indeed more likely to incorporate contemporary technology like the Internet, for our second review, we selected a nominee in the category of Best New Books, David Gordon's The Serialist: A Novel (Simon & Schuster).

Gordon says of himself in his blog:

> *"David Gordon was born in Queens and lives in New York City, with stops in New Jersey, London and Los Angeles along the way. He attended Sarah Lawrence College, holds an MA in English and Comparative Literature and an MFA in Fiction Writing, both from Columbia University, and has worked in film, fashion, publishing and pornography."* [9]

---

[9] http://www.davidgordonx.blogspot.com/

The book, like Gordon's thumbnail bio above, suggests a romp through popular culture. The protagonist is a writer attempting to survive despite the adverse impact of the Internet on publishing. Here is a bit of the flavor of the character and of the author's style:

> *"Still I'm a professional, of sorts, and since this is a Mystery/Suspense (shelve accordingly), I want to open in the classic style, with a hook, a real grabber that holds the reader hostage and won't let go, that will keep your sweaty little fingers feverishly turning the pages all night long. Something like this: It all began the morning when, dressed like my dead mother and accompanied by my fifteen-year-old schoolgirl business partner, I opened the letter from death row and discovered that a serial killer was my biggest fan."* [10]

In *The Serialist*, the Internet is a factor serving as a sort of symbol of the whirl increasingly overtaking our culture. The protagonist has lost much of his work as a writer because the Internet has destroyed the small serial magazines that were his primary market. He has been reduced to ghosting term papers for wealthy prep school students. But the Internet is not otherwise particularly important. In that way, it may be said to be a very realistic use of it—as we all know, sometimes it is useful, other times not.

Gordon's plot is not so much driven by a search to discover information as by events. The plot is pushed forward when things happen to the protagonist, in the style of the hapless detective of other writers. He is, by his nature, inherently out of control. Under such conditions, we do not much care about the author's use of the Internet. The book has some problems, but they are not relevant to the narrow focus of our inquiry; we will leave its fate to the judges of the Edgar awards.

In reading the Edgars systematically over three years now, it seems to me that there is a very big gap between authors nominated for the Best New Novel award and those nominated for the Best New Book. The former are often highly experienced heavyweights who have learned their craft by publishing books well into the double-digits, while the latter are very much beginners. Perhaps they are talented ones, like David Gordon, but nonetheless beginners.

---

[10] David Gordon, *The Serialist*, Loc 49-54 Kindle edition.

We have many books left to read before the Edgar Awards are announced in late April. At this point, we feel that, as P. D. James wrote in *Talking About Detective Fiction*, "... how far, if at all, these (changes (in technology) will actually affect the variety and type of fiction produced remains to be seen." [11]

As in all things, we are in a transitional period in the use of the Internet in detective fiction, and perhaps authors will adapt while refreshing the appeal of the genre.

---

[11] James, Loc 1612, (Kindle Edition)

Edgar Award Nominees, 2011, and the Impact of the Internet, Part II

Jeffrey Barlow

This is the second part of a recent article posted in *Interface* for March. [1] Because it is so highly opinionated on a topic regarding which many will argue, we treat it as an editorial and as a partial review of five books, each a nominee for the Edgar Allan Poe awards for best mystery novel in 2011. A sixth, Harlan Coben's *Caught* was reviewed earlier.

This editorial is related to a series of pieces analyzing the impact of the Internet through an examination of detective or mystery fiction. These works were selected because their quality had been affirmed by their nomination for the Edgar Allan Poe award. [2] As the winners for works published in 2011 will be named on April 28, we wanted to finish our discussion of them prior to that event.

Our methodology is a very simple one. We are interested, almost solely, in how the authors incorporate (or inappropriately ignore) the Internet in constructing their plots. This is a particularly useful approach for evaluating the impact of the Internet because, by its nature, the genre of mystery or detective fiction is most often focused on missing information. Usually that information is the identity of the perpetrator or criminal. The slang title for these works, "whodunit," is particularly appropriate.

The advent of the Internet has complicated mystery plotting because so much more information is available to both the sleuth and the reader. The reader is not likely to remain long interested in a detective who is too dumb to take the obvious first step in any research—going on line for related information. Authors then, either must utilize the Internet in an appropriate fashion, or ignore it convincingly.

We have now read all of the nominees for Best Novel, and most of those nominated for Best First Novel. We will comment upon this latter category after

---

[1] See "Edgar Award Nominees, 2011, and the Impact of the Internet" at: http://bcis.pacificu.edu/journal/article.php?id=779 Earlier related articles included: "Forward to a New Article Series: Detective Fiction and the Internet" http://bcis.pacificu.edu/journal/article.php?id=691 See also the review of C.J. Box, Blue Heaven, found at: http://bcis.pacificu.edu/journal/article.php?id=698 and the review of John Hart's work, The Last Child at: http://bcis.pacificu.edu/journal/article.php?id=728

[2] To see the Edgar award site, go to: http://www.theedgars.com/index.html

we know who the winner is. [3] Reading ten mystery novels between January 19 when the list was announced and the present was simply too much of a distraction from other work, perhaps because we so enjoy the project and the research.

There were six works nominated for the Best Novel of 2011:

- Harlan Coben's *Caught* (reviewed earlier)
- Tom Franklin's *Crooked Letter, Crooked Letter*
- Tana French's *Faithful Place.*
- Hallinan's *The Queen of Patpong*
- Steve Hamilton's *The Lock Artist*
- Laura Lippman's *I'd Know You Anywhere*

Each one of these works was good material to advance our understanding of the Internet because none was set in a time period before it developed. This is somewhat unusual when compared to previous lists of nominees, which almost always include at least one work set in an earlier historical period.

In our previous posting, we discussed Coben's *Caught* in tandem with a work from the list of Best First Work nominees, David Gordon's *The Serialist: A Novel.* [4] Of Coben's *Caught,* we wrote:

> *...so far as making good use of the Internet and constructing a plot around such timely issues as identity theft and on-line bullying...the work is certainly a major contender.*

Here we discuss the other works, and conclude with some generalizations and nominate our personal choice for the Edgar.

Two of the works, while not completely set in a time before the Internet, split the time frame. The earlier frame in which the crimes occur is pre-Internet. The later frame is a post-internet period when the earlier events are still having repercussions, in one case because the crime has not yet been solved.

Steve Hamilton's *The Lock Artist* is one of these. It is a fascinating work, if only, because the protagonist is certainly a unique voice: he is a mute world-class safe cracker. The metaphor of locks is consistent throughout: the narrator is mute because he was himself locked up under very traumatic circumstance, after which he is simply unable to speak. Hamilton brings alive the protagonist's strange world as well as explaining the technology of locks, and of opening them,

---

[3] The see the entire list of nominees, together with summaries and links to useful reviews, go to the appendix to this piece found at: http://bcis.pacificu.edu/journal/article.php?id=800
[4] Again, the review is found at: http://bcis.pacific"u.edu/journal/article.php?id=779

in an extremely lively fashion. Here is one brief paragraph—some of the descriptions go on for pages—

> *I set the back pin, started working my way to the front. All six pins set, go to the back again, set them all again. Here's where you have to be so careful, just enough tension to keep everything in place. One tiny bit too little and you lose it, one tiny bit too much and you can't feel it anymore. I worked through the second sets, got to the exact point I had gotten to before, with the locksmith laughing over my shoulder. This time I knew to keep going. Back pin again, third set. Work my way to the front. Damn, it was like balancing a house of cards. You have to keep going, but it gets harder and harder with each one, and one false move makes it all fall apart. I got almost to the end of the third sets, lost the tension, and felt the back pins start to give. So hard to keep the front pin set and to go back and fix the back. I let the whole thing go, took a deep breath, shook out my hands, and looked around the empty backyard.* [5]

This all occurs in 1999, at a time when there is no necessity of explaining the fact that the Internet is not a factor in transferring information. By the later time frame, 2008, the protagonist has been again locked away from access to the Internet. As interesting as it is, then, *The Lock Artist* is irrelevant to our analysis.

Tom Franklin's *Crooked Letter,* begins in 1979 when two boys are working out a very restricted version of friendship because one, Larry, is White, the other, Silas, is Black, and they live in a very racist southern culture. The White is accused of being responsible for the disappearance of a girl and his life is pretty much destroyed, though nothing can be proven due to the lack of a body or any other useful evidence. Their friendship ends and Silas continues on to become a successful college athlete and then Constable in his old hometown, getting his job over the Internet.

The time frame then jumps to an unspecified present when email is common and so is the Internet. Silas gets caught up once more in the old case involving Larry when other girls disappear. Because the setting remains deliberately isolated and by implication backward, we do not really think much about the Internet, nor about serial killer databases, or any other attribute of digital technology.

This is the second time in our process of analyzing mystery novels that we have seen what we now think of as the "Trope of the Backward South", in which the isolation of rural communities which are often also the scene of racially-motivated violence allows an author to finesse issues of Internet use by playing

---

[5] The Lock Artist: A Novel (Steve Hamilton)- Highlight Loc. 3589-3617

upon our stereotypes of rural areas. [6] This is, of course, ultimately illogical because the Internet is now ubiquitous, particularly in law enforcement agencies, no matter how isolated or Faulknerian the site.

Nonetheless, Tom Franklin's *Crooked Letter,* is very well done and fully worthy of its Edgar nomination.

Timothy Hallinan's *The Queen of Patpong* is one of two of the 2011 Edgar nominations which are set in a country other than the United States, in this case, Thailand. Admittedly I have a special interest in books set in Thailand, perhaps because I have been there just often enough to recognize locale and culture, but am not so familiar with it that I can really afford to be critical of the author's own understanding of the them.

One of the advantages of a Thai setting is that it gives an author an opportunity to present a radically non-Western worldview, particularly in matters of spirituality and sexuality. [7] Hallinan makes excellent use of these differences, presenting us with an ex-patriot protagonist, Poke Rafferty, who lives within a Thai family structure while remaining sufficiently American to be a useful foil to Thai values.

The book itself is excellent. The author's forte is character development and good use of the colorful locale as well as the very broad ethical structure of the locals, which permits them to move easily from high-class prostitute to loving and fiercely loyal girl friends or wives as useful to the plot.

Here the Internet is available, but not so available as to simplify the plot before the author can build suspense. The trope here is very much "Deus Ex Machina": the Internet is shut safely away until it can be trotted out at critical moments to resolve plot points or to carry them forward. The means of doing this is to have waiting in the off-stage area a very well-connected American intelligence agent who can, reluctantly, periodically feed critical information to the protagonist from databases to which only he has access.

We are trying, as best we can, to avoid plot spoilers here, but we can say that the identity of the criminal, a serial killer of Thai prostitutes, probably could have been resolved much earlier with a really thorough Google search. The emotionally satisfactory conclusion in which he is undone could have been much

[6] The first such use of this trope was in John Hart's work, The Last Child at: http://bcis.pacificu.edu/journal/article.php?id=728

[7] See, for example, our review of John Burdett's Bangkok Haunts at http://bcis.pacificu.edu/journal/2008/04/burdett.php. There we used the work to illuminate issues dealing with pornography as well as reviewing it for its use of the Internet.

more easily accomplished with the Thai equivalent of twitter than was the case. Nonetheless, this is another piece of excellent work.

Tana French's *Faithful Place* is, like Hallinan's *The Queen of Patpong,* set outside the United States, in this case, in Ireland. The protagonist is Frank Mackey, is a member of the Dublin Police forces' elite undercover squad. French, like all of the nominees for Best Book, has published more than one novel, and like Coben is a multiple nominee for the award.

French's setting of Ireland is not the happy Emerald Isle beloved of Irish-American lore, but a poverty stricken part of Dublin inhabited by radically dysfunctional families. The work open in 1985, when Rose, the youthful love of Mackey's life, disappears on the evening the two were to run away to London, free of their families and the suffocating puritanical culture of Ireland at that time. When she does not show up for their rendezvous, he chooses to believe that she simply decided that her chances were better without him, and did not truly love him as he loved her.

Twenty-two years later her body is found in the basement of the deserted tenement where they had regularly trysted, and where she had agreed to meet him. Now we are fully in the age of the Internet. Even Mackey's nine-year old daughter Holly is a skilled computer user who IM's with other children, and Mackey has access to all the digital panoply of police tools.

This is an excellent book. Ms. French moves as well as does any writer between male and female voices; [8] her protagonist Mackey is charming, devious, or brutal as required. The material culture of poverty-stricken Dublin is so well written that you feel you know even Mackey's marginally sane Irish catholic mother (his father, aided by drink, crossed over the borderline of sanity even before Rosy disappeared). The language of the characters is wonderful, my on-line Kindle dictionary while necessary, also failed repeatedly to turn up definitions of some of the language. [9]
The neighborhood itself becomes almost the chief suspect so mired is the crime in the complex relationships of its inhabitants. The crime is seemingly simple, but unraveling it requires working through the labyrinthine ties of family. At the end we feel as though we have read not simply a highly entertaining work of

---

[8] I have some caveats here: the voice or point of view, sometimes, I feel, switches gender. Through Mackay's eyes we get a very credible male voice, save when he discusses his mother; at this point I feel the point of view is female, as at a few other points in the mss, though this a minor inconsistency.

[9] A clear distinction, for example, between snogging, and shagging proved to be important in understanding the murder scene. Snogging is the American equivalent of "making-out", while shagging is pretty much the same in Ireland as in America. Either, it appears, is much more fraught with consequences in Ireland, particularly in a Catholic neighborhood, than in America.

fiction, but a tour de force exploration of the human condition, at least the Dublin humans' condition.

But now we come to the Internet. We have no problem dealing with the lack of the Internet at the time of the original crime. The denouement hinges in part on a paper message, which Rose may or may not have intended for Mckay. The early setting then gives us not only time for the many consequences of the crime to echo down the decades, but also explains why the two did not simply call each other…at one point it is said the families were in fact too poor to even have a land line.

Nor would the crime have been solved easier with the Internet than was in fact the case. The problem is the intervening of 22 years. Mackay sincerely believed that Rose was alive, so sincerely that his love for her interferes with his later marriage and other relationships. His wife leaves him, and later attributes this to his ongoing love for Rose, with whom she could not hope to compete. We know that he prowls police databases periodically looking for some evidence of either her death or her life.

It requires a considerable suspension of disbelief, however, to imagine that for 22 years Rose had escaped being somehow referenced on the Internet. This is particularly true because it had been her intention when she planned to run away to make a career in the music business in London. The only possible reason for her complete disappearance simply had to be that she was dead. Once that realization occurred, a simple search of the area she had last planned to be would have turned up her body quite easily as another clue was found pointing to her probable death.

This painstaking—even nitpicking---analysis on my part however, may tell us about the impact of the Internet, but it in no way diminishes our enjoyment of Tana French's *Faithful Place.* It is a very worthy work and Ms. French is a wonderful writer. This was the first of her works I have read and I intend to ultimately read all of them.

Now we come to Laura Lippman's *I'd Know You Anywhere.* Lippman, like Coben and French, is a multiple Edgar winner and the author of at least 19 works. *I'd Know You Anywhere* displays a very accomplished and experienced writer at the top of her game. It also shows a marvelous use of the Internet.

The protagonist, Eliza Benedict, had been kidnapped and held for six weeks in 1985 by a serial killer, Walter Bowman, and was the only surviving victim of his spree. Now, in the apparent present, he contacts her from his cell on death row. He has seen a contemporary picture of her in a magazine to which he has access, and tracked her down. Given our limited purposes in this review, it is possible to avoid revealing too much about his motives, but they are one of the issues upon which the plot hinges.

The author uses Internet searches by the protagonist to unfold the back-story, which we do not believe we have seen before. By searching her maiden name, she turns up the past details of her life, and the reader is quickly brought up to speed on the earlier relationship between her and Bowen. This is necessary because she herself has little or no memory of the earlier trauma. This is a very clever device, which facilitates a plot that can take radical twists and turns without the reader at any point calling foul. We know what the Internet knows, and do not know what the Eliza no longer knows.

Eliza is a very competent computer user. Her use of the Internet is consistent through the book without being spectacular. She is not a highly wired heroine who can find information the rest of us could not. For example, she has a very troubled 13 year-old, Isobel (Iso), whom she has begun to suspect needs greater surveillance than she has hitherto been given, particularly when a serial killer of young women has suddenly reentered the family's lives:

> *Eliza had installed spyware on the computer and monitored Iso's IM sessions, which appeared benign enough. Now Iso was pushing for her own phone, but Eliza wasn't sure if she could track text messages. She would have to seek the advice of other mothers—assuming she eventually made friends with any.* [10]

The author is very conscious of differing periods of Internet use and repeatedly plays successfully upon changes between periods. Early in the period following her kidnapping a not very talented writer had written a true-crime expose sort of book in which he had speculated that she had been not a victim but the female member of a spree-killing team, perhaps even the initiator of the crime for which Bowen was convicted. She once had hoped that her story would die down and she could live a normal life. Her husband tells her, however:

> *But his book is out there. Nothing really disappears anymore. Once, that kind of true-crime crap would be gone forever, gathering dust in a handful of secondhand bookstores, pulped by the publishers. Now, with online bookstores and eBay and POD technology, it's a computer click away for anyone who remembers your original name. For all you know, he's uploaded it to Kindle, sells it for ninety-nine cents a pop.* [11]

The Internet, in Lippman's work, is very much a part of the environment. When we might turn to it, so does the protagonist. Neither the central mystery nor its

---

[10] I'd Know You Anywhere: A Novel (Laura Lippman)- Highlight Loc. 209-11
[11] I'd Know You Anywhere: A Novel (Laura Lippman)- Highlight Loc. 501-4

unraveling depends in any terribly critical way on the Internet. We are not left with any questions as to why the protagonist had missed easily retrievable information.

If we were to give a "Berglund Best Use of the Internet in Mystery Fiction" to any of the Edgar nominees for 2011, it would go to Harlan Coben first, and secondly, to Laura Lippman. If I were to guess at the eventual winner of the Best Book award, however, I would pick Tana French's *Faithful Place.* It is a very successful traditional sort of mystery set in such an unusual place among fascinating characters, and so well-written that it will be difficult to ignore, I believe.

Conclusion

So what have we learned about the impact of the Internet in this series using high-quality mystery novels as our research materials? First, our belief that the Internet cannot be ignored is born out by our survey. When we are looking for it, at least, its absence can be painfully obvious, and may reveal weaknesses or contrivances in plotting. Even an excellent work, like French's *Faithful Place* can be seen to have a weakness at its heart.

Authors have developed several recognizable tropes to work around the damage which ignoring the Internet might do to their plots. One is what we are now calling the "Trope of the Backward South," in which novels can be set in isolated backwoods areas which somewhat alleviate the expectation of a darned good Google search casting light upon plot issues. When we are careening up and down gravel roads looking out for racist rednecks, somehow our expectations are lowered, along with our critical faculties, as in last year's nominee, John Hart's work, *The Last Child*, and this year's nominee, Tom Franklin's *Crooked Letter.*

Another trope is a very old one, familiar to even ancient Greek theater audiences, the "Deus Ex Machina" in which a god, in this case, the Internet, unexpectedly intervenes at key moments to solve critical questions and carry the plot forward while being mysteriously absent at others. This was the case in last year's nominee, *Blue Heaven*, by C.J. Box. Box also threw in a variant on the "Trope of the Backward South," which we might call the "Trope of the Noble West," in which the enemy is modernity, which threatens to corrupt a western community and its cowboy detective. In this case, the detective's computer-enabled sidekick cannot get internet-derived critical information to him because of a lack of good phone service. When service is available, the god magically descends.

In this year's nominee, *The Queen of Patpong* by Timothy Hallinan, there is a similar working of the two tropes. Because we don't know exactly how Internet savvy Thai hookers are, we suspend disbelief a la the Backward South. And a handy but reluctant intelligence agent periodically descends into the plot with necessary information to unravel it.

None of these, of course, are bad books. Not only are they all engrossing reads, but also they are well plotted by all conventional standards, and they have, after all, each been nominated for the highest award in mystery or detective fiction.

It is possible, however, to write an excellent mystery novel while making good or appropriate use of the Internet. Both Harlan Coben's *Caught*, and Laura Lippman's *I'd Know You Anywhere* do so. In this survey, the success at using the Internet ranges from rather contrived attempts to avoid doing so by use of the tropes discussed above, to the spectacularly successful use by Harlan Coben and the very naturalistic and utilitarian use by Laura Lippman. Perhaps this ultimately shows that the impact of the Internet is progressing in mystery fiction as in most other aspects of modern life, but also that it threatens some of our old practices.

Jason Ohler's Digital Community: Digital Citizen

Review by Richard Tinsen and Michael Charles

Digital Community: Digital Citizen takes the reader down a three-part path to digital citizenry. First is a description of how digital citizenship fits within the evolution of citizenship and community; second is a discussion of learning to see technology and its impact on our society, and third is a practical discussion of how to create a good digital community through good citizenry. The 12 chapters are easy to read, well organized, and include a rare combination of "big picture" perspectives and practical classroom applications.

Part I contains some of the best parts of the book as Ohler presents his ideas in an historical context. For example, in Chapter Two, Ohler gives "An extremely short history of civilization" [1] that traces evolution of the modern state starting with the Greek city-states. This leads to an insight into the challenges of citizenship independent of the influence of technology and shows citizenship as a concept that has been evolving for over 2000 years. It is fundamental to the concept of citizenship that it has, and will, continue to evolve.

His first and third points are particularly germane to the educator; citizenship requires individual virtuous behavior, and it requires education. The importance of virtuous behavior is addressed again in Part Three of the book, but it is a critical aspect of the social obligation of the educator. The second important concept described in Part I is the inseparable connection between citizenship and community.

Ohler's concept of community is similar to the anthropological description of culture and shares the same attributes. As a culture we have both the introspective challenge to define who we are as well as a contemplative requirement to define who we want to be. We need to understand both the current and desired behaviors of our community as a prelude to defining and teaching "virtuous behavior".

---

[1] Jason Ohler, "An Extremely Short History of Citizenship" in *Digital Community: Digital Citizen* (Thousand Oaks, CA: Corwin, 2010), 28-36.

The theme of Part II is that "in order to help students become effective digital citizens, we must help them see technology that is largely invisible to them". [2] Ohler points out that this is exactly the opposite of the advice given by most in the field of educational technology, who believe that the technology needs to become less visible as the focus turns to enabling better learning of the use of technology. But as a student of Marshal McLuhan, Ohler has a sharp eye for the ways that technology impacts our lives, both positively and negatively, and he believes that students need to be "actively engaged in deconstructing technology and making connections between what it does and how it connects us". [3] His recommendations are very much in line with the National Educational Technology Standard 5: "Students understand human, cultural, and societal issues related to technology and practice legal and ethical behavior". [4] But his recommendations that technology be an object of study itself may strike many practicing educators as laudable, but undoable, given the current crowded nature of the curriculum. He says more about this issue in Part III.

In Part III, Ohler returns to the issues of values. He even admits surprise that the "my journey would ultimately bring me to the topic of character education. Yet in hindsight, it seems inevitable." [5] He considers several different abhorrent behaviors that are current issues in discussions of the Internet. They run from cyberbullying to factition (a person who distorts fact and fiction for the betterment of their own personal agenda) but his most pertinent observation is that we are responding to these issues individually. He concludes that "We need a whole-school approach to behavior that sets the entirety of being digitally active within an overall ethical and behavior context-character education for the digital age." [6]

An ideal school board is created as a context for addressing the five agenda items that are identified as necessary for creating an environment nurturing to good digital citizenship.

The first agenda item is helping teachers understand their own core ethics. Ohler recognizes the potential minefield that teachers would encounter, but the school board will wholeheartedly support the teacher in this new role (remember this is an *ideal* school board). The role of teacher as an ethical coach is introduced with an admonishment to "understand our own ethical cores".

---

[2] Ohler, *Digital Community*, 108.
[3] Ohler, *Digital Community*, 91.
[4] "NETS for Students 2007", International Society for Technology in Education, accessed January 5, 2011, http://www.iste.org/standards/nets-for-students/nets-student-standards-2007.aspx
[5] Ohler, *Digital Community*, 139.
[6] Ohler, *Digital Community*, 145.

Ohler's use of the term "ethical cores" seems redundant and confusing. Ohler himself recognizes the common confusion between morality, ethics, and values; he even dedicates a sidebar [7] to his own definition, but he does not seem to consistently use the terms. Later, in chapter 10, additional terms "core ethical values and supportive performance values" are added without explanation. Perhaps consistent usage of the term *ethics* as being non-temporal and collective would have clarified his message of digital citizenry being a modern application in which we need to define a moral framework.

The second agenda item is to take "A crash course in kids". This will help us to understand the difference in the digital community from the real life community and also to better understand childhood brain research and how that impacts moral development. The teacher uses the newly discovered ethical compass to teach the students a moral roadmap. Students can be involved in this process by taking responsibility for how technology is used and maintained in their own schools. For example, students involved in projects such as Gen-Yes are asked to solve technical problems *and* provide their own perspectives on issues of digital citizenship. [8]

Moral development inevitably leads to the need for character education in agenda item three. "The Eleven Principles of Effective Character Education" [9] are presented and modified with a digital age focus. Principle 5 in that list can be updated with a digital focus (listed in italics): The schools sets clear expectations for students to engage in moral action in terms of civility, personal responsibility, good sportsmanship, helping others, and service to school and community *within local, global, and digital communities.* [10]

The fourth item on the agenda addresses important issues on supporting the goals of the first three. Literacy has long been understood as a requirement in an effective Democracy. We need to expand our understanding of literacy to include the demands of the new media. There are many more avenues in the digital world and some are less safe than others. Ohler points out that we must "develop literacy not just with digital tools but also about digital tools". The skills to open a browser are analogous to the skills to open a book. The real value in each is the ability to understand content and evaluate the accuracy. Even more important is that we move students past literacy and into fluency in areas such as solution development, information use, creativity and others. [11]

---

[7] Ohler, *Digital Community*, 157.
[8] "GenYES - Student Powered Technology Integration", Generation YES Corporation, Accessed January 3, 2011 from http://genyes.org/programs/genyes
[9] *"11 Principles of Effective Character Education",* Character education Partnership. Accessed December 30, 2010 from http://www.character.org/elevenprinciples
[10] Ohler, *Digital Community*, 203.
[11] Ohler, *Digital Community*, 215.

The final agenda item addresses the infrastructure required for digital citizenry and the key role played by IT departments. There is an interesting suggestion that each member of the IT department spend a half-hour in the classroom every week (remember this is an *ideal* school board).

The book is at its strongest when it makes connections between the special requirements of the digital citizen and the need for character education in the curriculum. A good case is made for the social importance of high character in the digital world. In addition, a strong case is made that character education, which has a strong tradition in US education tracing back to Washington and Jefferson, might be a key to opening up the narrowing of the curriculum brought about by No Child Left Behind and related policies. "The NCLB approach to schooling stands in stark contrast to other movement in education...such as 21st Century Learning Skills, which emphasized innovation, creativity, *citizenship*, and learning in a social context" [12] (emphasis mine).

The reader may find the endless lists that Ohler compiles in this book a bit tiring, and his penchant for creating new words in the McLuhan tradition (e.g. Partycipation as a synonym for Web 2.0 tools) may tire some readers. But for a wide ranging and practical discussion of issues of digital citizenship appropriate for educators in particular, one would be hard pressed to find a better read.

---

[12] Ohler, *Digital Community*, 191.

Bibliography

Character Education Partnership, *11 Principles of Effective Character Education"*, Accessed December 30, 2010 from http://www.character.org/elevenprinciples

Generation YES, "GenYES - Student Powered Technology Integration", Accessed January 3, 2011 from http://genyes.org/programs/genyes .

International Society for Technology in Education, "NETS for Students 2007", Accessed January 5, 2011, http://www.iste.org/standards/nets-for-students/nets-student-standards-2007.aspx .

Jason Ohler, *Digital Community: Digital Citizen.* Thousand Oaks, CA: Corwin, 2010.

Robert Glenn Howard's *Digital Jesus*

The Making of a New Christian Fundamentalist Community on the Internet. New York: New York University Press, 2011

Review by Jeffrey Barlow

The impact of the Internet upon religion has been an ongoing study for us at the Berglund Center. Here we review an important new book, Robert Glenn Howard's *Digital Jesus,* which tells us a great deal about the Internet, as well as much about one specific form of religion, Protestant Fundamentalism. [1]

As always in reviewing works about religion, we are aware that the topic itself is often of interest primarily to those who already hold religious values similar to those of the author. After all, religion is one of the two topics verboten in polite company, the other being politics. However, to ignore this book would be to fail to understand a great deal of value, particularly the connection between these two black topics and the Internet itself.

Robert G. Howard is extremely well qualified to discuss these issues. He is Director of Digital Studies at the University of Wisconsin-Madison and the author of twenty works on religion or spirituality, with special reference to the Internet and/or apocalyptic cults. He has been studying Fundamentalism—defined below—in electronic environments since well before the development of the World Wide Web. Consequently, he is almost uniquely able to analyze the changes that are made in religious practices and beliefs as electronic communication developed from the early use of Newsgroups through to the present Web 2.0, and all media in between.

Howard's own religious beliefs will be of interest to some. His objectivity, however, is such that all we can say is that he was raised as a Baptist. The heart of his own spirituality is an Augustinian approach to *caritas*, sometimes translated as charity or "Brotherly Love". [2] Howard holds this value to be at the heart of Christian belief. Consequently, some of the Fundamentalist communities that he is discussing here would disqualify him as incapable of a full understanding of their communities—or worse, possibly even demonic or satanic in his intentions—because he himself is not a Fundamentalist.

---

[1] We previously have reviewed Daniel Henrich's *Internet Evangelism in the 21st Century* at: http://bcis.pacificu.edu/journal/article.php?id=763. Earlier, we reviewed Peter D. Hershock's work, *Reinventing the Wheel: A Buddhist Response to the Information Age* at: http://bcis.pacificu.edu/journal/article.php?id=185.

[2] See discussion at Howard, pp 168-170.

Those of such an opinion who refused to read the work would, however, miss an opportunity to better understand their own beliefs and the relationship between them and digital communications. In our view, Howard successfully maintains a perspective which is both objective and compassionate.

Among the many strengths of *Digital Jesus* is a very close understanding of the historical development of modern Christianity. Howard traces the notion of Fundamentalism back to the early twentieth century. At that time, four core beliefs were described as "Fundamental," initially in England, and later in the United States. These are:

1. A belief in biblical literalism
2. A belief in the experience of spiritual rebirth
3. A belief in the importance of evangelism
4. And a belief in "End Times" interpretations of biblical prophecy [3]

These beliefs, by their nature and the degree to which they deviated from "Main Line" Christianity, that is, the major Protestant denominations, tended to isolate believers from their local communities and were largely confined to small sects often dominated by charismatic individuals.

With the development of digital communications, however, believers were able to reach out to each other in electronic environments. A number of consequences flowed from these new environments.

First, it became possible for "virtual" communities to form. Another of the strengths of Howard's analysis is a very precise understanding of the term "virtual." To him, virtual means not merely digital (in the sense of an avatar in an online game) nor visible by its corporeal existence, but rather "manifest by its effects." [4]

This distinction is of considerable importance for digital Fundamentalist communities. From being small communities centered about a physical church and a charismatic leader, they have become decentralized online communities with no particular leader. They exist only online, and without a hierarchical structure.

Many might think that this change would ultimately destroy a religious community. Howard, however, argues that this community is not unlike the very early Christian communities in which worship consisted of fellowship and a public profession of shared beliefs, an *Ekklesia*. [5] Rather than being fragmented

---

[3] Howard, p. 8.

[4] Howard, p. 12-13.

[5] See discussion at p. 11.

or endangered, Fundamentalists living in communities too small to support churches appropriate to their beliefs can now gather online. It is, Howard argues, precisely their communications regarding their core beliefs that constitutes their worship; they have become a *virtual ekklesia*.

These ekklesia have changed in another important way: they have become *vernacular*—a folk response outside the recognized institutional framework of even the Protestant Fundamentalism in which they began. Each website develops its own special forms of both content and procedure, and taken together they are thoroughly de-centered. [6]

Howard traces the development of the virtual ekklesia from early forms beginning with Newsgroups, which he began studying in 1994, through Email Lists or Listservs, onto the World Wide Web, and now, onto Web 2.0. Each of these technologies has had its own impact, and Howard's analysis of the development of these forms begins with ARPANET in 1979. [7] Scholars of the Internet will find Howard very well grounded in the work of familiar authorities and his substantial index is a litany of great names in Anthropology as well as in Internet studies. [8]

The impact of Web 2.0, the participatory web, is critical to the development of vernacular Fundamentalism. In earlier groups, which were usually open to any participant willing to observe minimal rules (no cursing, no flaming, etc.), anyone was welcome. In such open environments, Fundamentalists were often uncomfortable; they wanted to discuss questions that were based in beliefs that were not widely shared and hence often attacked, gently or otherwise.

The earlier forms of the Internet—web pages—were more useful than Newsgroups because Fundamentalists could post content supporting their own particular views in controlled environments. However, these could be participatory in only a minimal sense. Communications were usually of necessity one-to-one via email. While these were affirming to believers, it was Web 2.0 that created the virtual ekklesia. Now, using various forms of BBS (Bulletin Boards) or commenting systems, believers could aggregate their opinions and, by requiring pledges of fidelity to core beliefs, control access. If individuals did

---

[6] The curious reader may want to pause here and go to such sites as: http://prophecycorner.theforeverfamily.com/; http://www.acts17-11.com/studies.html; http://www.mt.net/~watcher/; http://raptureforums.com/ A Google search on http://www.google.com/search?q=End+Times&ie=utf-8&oe=utf-8&aq=t&rls=org.mozilla:en-US:official&client=firefox-a will turn up millions of references to such sites.

[7] That is, the government network which was the precursor to later more widespread forms of digital online communication. See Howard's analysis of these changes in chapter 3, "Networking the Apocalypse," especially at pp 48-9.

[8] Howard also teaches in the Department of Communication Arts at Wisconsin.

not conform to both appropriate behaviors and appropriate beliefs, they could be, and often were, removed from the digital community.

Howard has well gone beyond his initial careful longitudinal study of Christian Fundamentalism online. In 1999 he began a series of intensive interviews. He has interviewed all of the important figures among these communities, and his careful even-handed treatment does a great deal to humanize them for the reader, going far to overcome what may be our own prejudices.

Howard understands the major participants not only as individuals, but also as a network. He develops careful distinctions as to types of online discourse, ranging from "authoritarian" ("Believe me because I am channeling God Almighty!") to a less authoritative and participatory model (This is what I think; what do you think about this?).

While Howard seems to us to be compassionate and objective, this does not mean that he does not think critically. Underlying his analysis is an awareness of some of the harsher realities behind virtual Fundamentalism. Fundamentalism has long been associated, in the view of many scholars and of mainstream churches, with various forms of prejudice and intolerant behavior.

Howard argues that, to the present at least, the ability to aggregate in vernacular Fundamentalist groups has probably strengthened the tendency of these groups to shut themselves off from contrary opinions. As he points out, if there is not some form of enforcing agreement, such groups would quickly collapse into welters of disagreements, and Howard discusses specific examples of just this phenomenon. [9]

Because of what the author refers to as their "radical certainty" ("I know this is true because I have experienced it, not because I can document or demonstrate it..."). Fundamentalists are sometimes prone to attack and denounce those who deviate from their own beliefs. Their beliefs are thus "self-sealing" and tend to isolate them.

Howard believes that such cloistered behavior easily grows harmful to those who deliberately isolate themselves from contrary opinion. In this environment, for example, what outsiders might view as very strange beliefs easily flourish. Howard's fascinating chapter on the 9/11 attacks as a purported harbinger of the apocalypse is very interesting reading. The frequent connections between Fundamentalist beliefs, political conservatism, and fringe conspiracy beliefs are easier to understand after reading Howard's thorough work.

---

[9] Howard, p 147.

Howard believes, or perhaps better, hopes, that many younger Christians who have been raised with the Internet have not only a commitment to the four core beliefs, but also to the importance of open communication. These, he says, indicate that tolerance is a growing phenomenon. [10]

Howard's *Digital b* is fascinating for a great many reasons, and will greatly advance the careful reader's understanding of many topics, including the impact of the Internet, the development and nature of online communities, the history of Fundamentalist Christianity, and the nature of current American vernacular communities. We think it well worth reading, and worth drawing to the attention of Christian friends and family members.

[10] Howard, pp 167-8.

Tim Elmore's. Generation iY: *Our Last Chance to Save Their Future.*

Review by Jeffrey Barlow

This book is very like Longfellow's little girl, who "When she was good, She was very good indeed. But when she was bad she was horrid." [1] First, the very good.

Judging from this particular work, the author, Dr. Tim Elmore, writes largely in support of his speaking engagements. [2] This is not uncommon in certain sorts of entrepreneurial operations. Elmore works as a motivational speaker, focusing on the development of leadership. As his biography proclaims, he has worked with a number of corporations and spoken at many universities, and in, all told, more than thirty countries. [3]

The author's credentials stem in large part from his sheer productivity. He has written more than twenty books, most of them focused, it appears, on living a Christian life of the sort that is conducive to developing not only excellent character but also leadership skills. Generation iY drew our attention because it seems to be one of many works discussing the changes wrought in younger generations by the impact of the Internet. We thought it worth analyzing, assuming it to be one of the large number of cautionary works—in large part because of the subtitle "Our Last Chance to Save Their Future," —which bemoan the loss of everything from attention spans to resistance to pornography on the part of those exposed to the Internet.

We were wrong in this assumption. The author is concerned about the Internet, no mistake in that; the work is full of cautionary tales of damage done to the unwary, such as addiction to video games and/or pornography, rapid weight gain, poor eyesight, etc., etc. [4] However, the author's approach is much more nuanced than many that are sometimes encountered. Dr. Elroy believes that the generation born between 1984 and 2002, which he calls "iY," is also very promising, very socially concerned, tolerant, quick to learn, ambitious, and

---

[1] http://wonderingminstrels.blogspot.com/2001/07/there-was-little-girl-henry-wadsworth.html

[2] See his page at: http://timelmore.com/index.php?option=com_content&view=article&id=47&Itemid=27

[3] It fails, however, to mention the source of the degree which justifies his use of the title "Dr." He lists Azusa Pacific University, a Christian school in southern California on his resume, and perhaps he has a D. Min. from there.

[4] See the dismaying list at p. 22.

confident. [5] Moreover, when all is said and done, they are all we have got, so far as future leaders are concerned.

The value of the book, I think, is precisely that, while highly concerned about the Internet, it nonetheless sees it as potentially extremely positive, like the iY generation themselves. The author puts constant stress on the importance of understanding this generation, parenting them closely, and helping them through the challenges facing them in what to me seems to be a relatively objective and useful fashion. I think that reading the book and its many cautions and such suggestions as "action steps" to positively impact children [6] might have improved my own parenting and teaching skills, particularly so far as dealing with the impact of media upon children.

The work, like the author himself, makes excellent use of the Internet. Each chapter ends with suggestions for clicking upon his massive web site, injunctions to post comments, get involved, receive additional printed materials—all sophisticated interactive approaches to the subject.

However, that having been said, the work has many faults. It is overwritten to a painful extent. It is full of overly folksy tales of individual youth and their well-nigh miraculous recoveries from the threats facing them. Many of these stories are so obvious and naïve that when we read in his acknowledgement his thanks to his editor, who trimmed the mss down from its original 350 pages to the current 215, we too want to get down on our knees, overwhelmed with gratitude.

The work is repetitive in the extreme. The author uses the common business book strategy of making frequent early notices of material to be introduced later, introduces the material itself, and sometimes makes later references back to the same point. This is perhaps an appropriate approach for a motivational speech, but a wasteful strategy for a printed book.

[5] P. 35.

[6] Summary at p. 69.

The research supporting the work is amateurish. The author relies very heavily on one or two sources for his major points in each chapter, and only those that support his own rather narrow point of view—no hint of controversy is found in this work. Some of these are useful materials written by experts in the field bearing upon the author's analysis, but many are from stories flashed on network news or taken from the pages of U.S.A. Today. When he does make personal claims to authority, it is usually derived from his encounters—in his leadership seminars and speaking engagements—with thousands of the youth whom he discusses here. These references are very unsystematic and often ultimately supported by homilies as opposed to serious research or a grasp of scholarship in the field.

The author has a curious take on the root source of the problems facing the youth about whom he is concerned. At no point does he really condemn advertising or all the panoply of tools of a consumer economy—after all, he hopes, we think, to one day advise these very same corporations on how best to employ these youth and to assist the corporations in honing the leadership skills of their workforces. But he does occasionally caution about the evils of the material world, and the importance of not getting entirely caught up in it. He also has an understanding of the pressures generated by an increasingly troubled economy and its impact on families.

Some of his discussion of the sources of the peril facing youth, in addition to unregulated use of the Internet, may strike some as idiosyncratic. He believes, for example, that the physical results of particular synthetic chemicals in the environment are not only impacting the attention span by producing ADHD (attention deficit hyperactivity disorder), but also feminizing males.

We have some particular concern about his stealthy approach to his own obviously deeply held Christian values. He never really uses any Christian keywords, but there is a series of code-like references intended, we believe, to signal to readers and potential employers that the author enthusiastically plays on God's Team. We assume that he does not want to alienate potential audiences, so he chooses to position himself as simply deeply concerned. We suspect that when appearing before many of the church groups, which seem to account for much of his audience, he is much more partisan in his approach. [7]

---

[7] We are basing this judgment on the forward to his book, and the blurbs on various others, as well as his own web postings.

We also are disturbed by his failure to deal with national cultures. So far as he is concerned, all the youth of this generation in the world share the same problems—a Palestinian youth, a Somali refugee, and a middle-American yuppie are all equally generation iY. This is, we think, naïve.

On balance, we believe that there is a definite audience for this work, and for the author's other books and speeches. We think that many who might otherwise simply see the Internet as the Devil's Digital Workshop could well be led to a better understanding of the complexities of modern life, and particularly of the challenges facing the young. However, many others, particularly those wanting to achieve a serious understanding of the Internet based in expertise and research, will find it, well, horrid.

Editorials – Volume 11

Jeffrey Barlow – *Google's Ngram Viewer*
http://bcis.pacificu.edu/interface/?p=379

Jeffrey Barlow – *Peaceful Evolution in China and the World Wide Web. Part IV: The Internet as the Bulwark of Chinese Democracy?*
http://bcis.pacificu.edu/interface/?p=304

Jeffrey Barlow – *Studying China Online: Editorial Review*
http://bcis.pacificu.edu/interface/?p=506

Google's Ngram Viewer

Editorial by Jeffrey Barlow

Google has brought out applications and various cloud-related services so very quickly that it is sometimes quite easy to miss them. Google's Ngram Viewer is such an application from late 2010.

Ngram is simultaneously a service, a site, an application, and a search device—all summed up in the name "Viewer". It surveys the many millions of books in the humanities scanned and indexed to date by Google. The Viewer permits the user to scan for strings of up to five words found in any or all of the works in a search process largely defined by the user, and in a variety of languages, too.

Here is Google's explanation of the Ngram Viewer:

> *"Since 2004, Google has digitized more than 15 million books worldwide. The datasets we're making available today to further humanities research are based on a subset of that corpus, weighing in at 500 billion words from 5.2 million books in Chinese, English, French, German, Russian, and Spanish. The datasets contain phrases of up to five words with counts of how often they occurred in each year."* [1]

There are many potential uses for such a search device. Students of intellectual or cultural history, for example, are often going to be interested in the occurrence and distribution of particular terms or ideas over long time periods.

For example, we are currently assisting a senior history major with her thesis research. The topic is submarines and the policies adopted in an attempt to control them via treaty agreements.

One of the student's major arguments after initial research is that the submarine was quickly associated with criminal behavior, as it began to develop in the late nineteenth and early twentieth centuries, because it violated Romantic traditions of warfare. These were basically related to chivalry and held that

---

[1] http://booksearch.blogspot.com/2010/12/find-out-whats-in-word-or-five-with.html?utm_source=feedburner&utm_medium=feed&utm_campaign=Feed%3A+blogspot%2FCjSP+%28Book+ Search%3A+Inside+Google+Book+Search%29
See also a very positive description of the Ngrams at:
http://online.wsj.com/article/SB10001424052748704073804576023741849922006.html
Yet more detailed analysis can be found at:
http://www.sciencemag.org/content/early/2010/12/15/science.1199644

gentlemen did not read each other's mail, nor would they kill civilians or attack from ambush as did submarines, etc.

Furthermore, the student believes, the technological development of the submarine eventually outran attempts to craft appropriate policy, and by World War II, war had grown so terrible that the submarine seemed no worse than many other hitherto inhuman weapons. In short, by 1945 the Romantic vision of warfare was pretty much dead.

These are not, of course, easy arguments to prove or demonstrate. Most arguments in intellectual history usually must rest on evidence drawn from one or more influential writers, and always leave upon questions as to how typical or widespread that particular perspective in fact was. With the Ngram Viewer, we have an opportunity to discuss the occurrence of any given search string on the basis of a large sample.

In an effort to improve our own understanding of these issues, and to learn to use Ngram, we turned to it. I first ran a search on the word "submarine" in Ngram's English-language corpus. Here were the results: [2] [following page]

---

2 http://ngrams.googlelabs.com/graph?content=submarine&year_start=1800&year_end=2000&corpus=0&smoothing=3

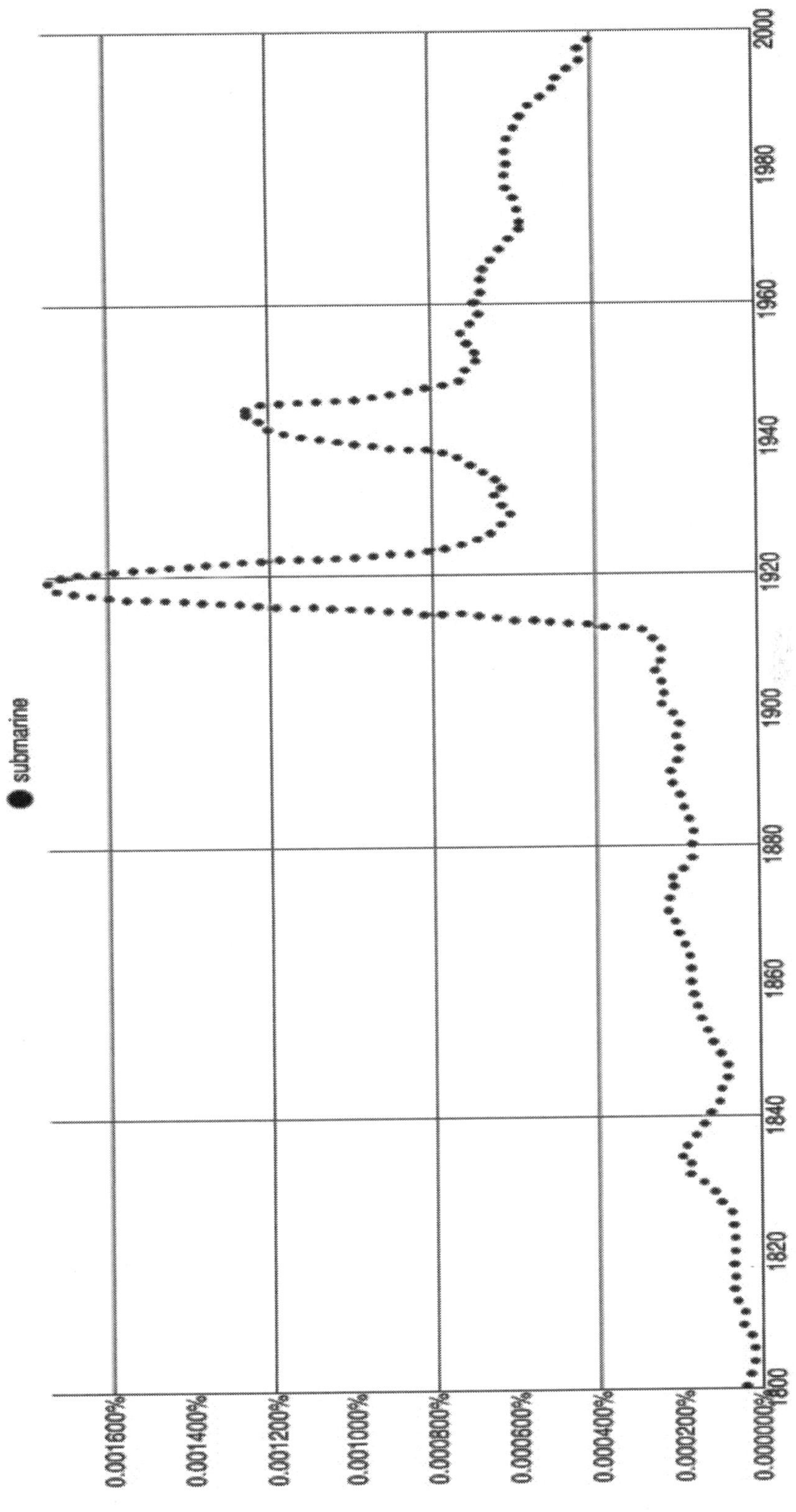

Figure 1 Ngram Graph of the Word "submarine"

This graph [previous page] nicely demonstrates two important points of which the student was already aware: concern about submarine warfare peaked in the early period of the First World War, and again in the Second World War, but the use of the term was apparently much more frequent in the first period. This is possible support for the student's position that the submarine had pretty much lost its criminal aura by the end of World War II.

However, we also learn some of the limitations of an Ngram search. When we click on the graph we can go to the list of books where the term was used. Here we find out that there are various meanings of *submarine*, which includes not only the naval weapon, but also the undersea telegraph cable. So we must narrow our search to see if the first simple conclusion---that apparently there were more works published which discussed submarines in WW I than in WW II---is accurate or that it may be some statistical freak resulting from searching a word used in a variety of contexts.

So now we run the search "submarine warfare." Here are the results: [3] [following page]

[3] http://ngrams.googlelabs.com/graph?content=submarine+warfare&year_start=1800&year_end=2000&corpus=0&smoothing=3

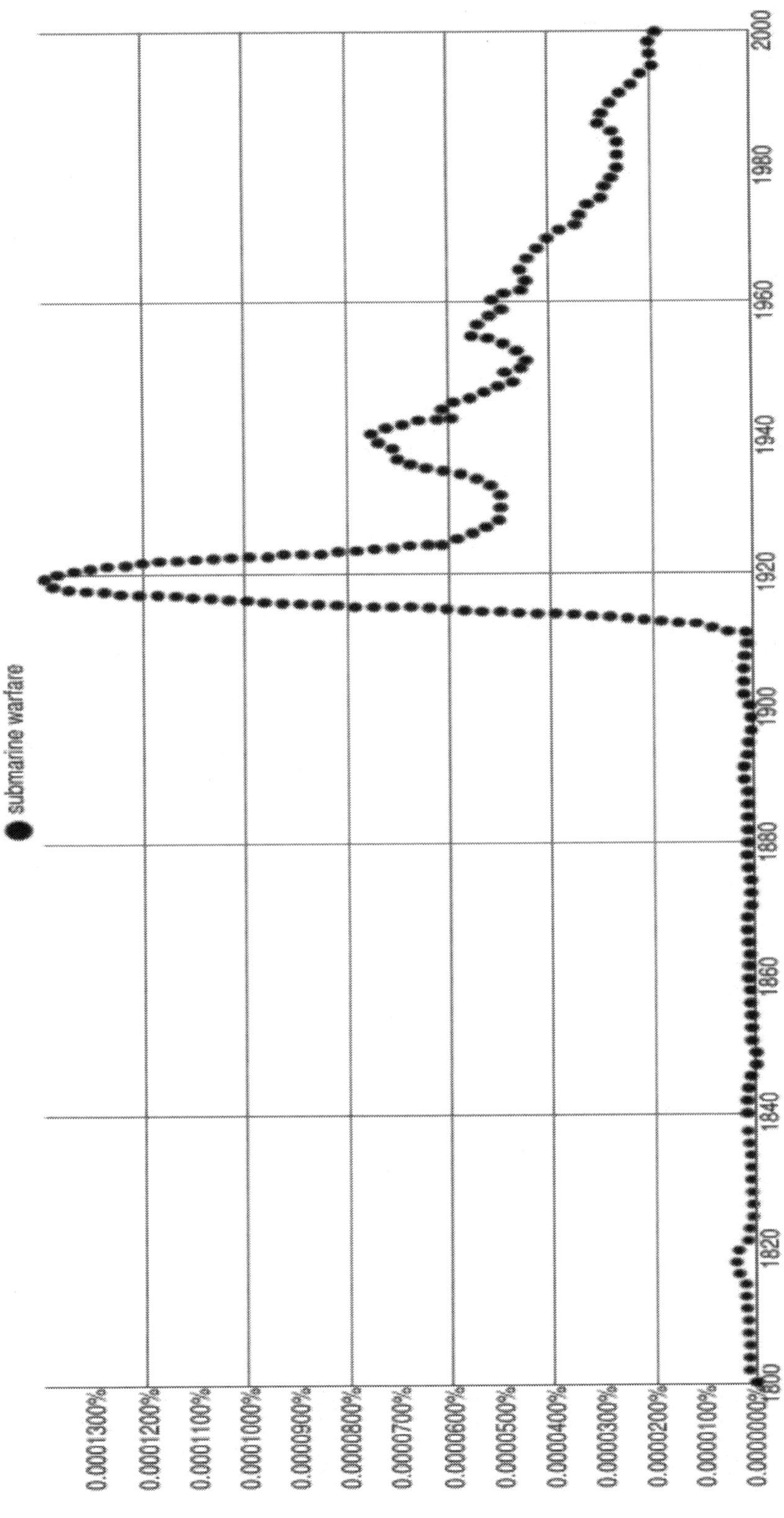

Figure 2 Ngram Graph of Words "submarine warfare"

We have now filtered out the references, we assume, to everything but submarine warfare. We see that our initial conclusions seem to still stand. Though there are some fluctuations in the percentage of books which utilized the term, the respective peaks are still visible.

This new search is interesting however, because there is a bump in usage between 1812 and 1820. This is very early for submarine warfare, and we want to see what is causing the bump. We refine the search at the above link by going into the frame 1800-1917 at the foot of the graph. We then further refine the search in the next page, [4], [2] by undertaking a more sophisticated search that enables us to sort the documents by years published.

This leads us to a number of books from the period of 1812-1820, most referring to the proposal of Robert F. Fulton to develop submarines for use by the British government against Napoleon. This, incidentally, is something of which neither myself nor the student doing the actual work was aware.

Now we want to take advantage of the language filter on Ngram to see if there are differences between German and English language sources. This is because, as has long been known, Germany made good use of the submarine earlier than any other power, and it was precisely the degree to which it violated Romantic notions of war that caused Woodrow Wilson, among others, to condemn Germany for its use. Germany, in short, may have been much less prejudiced toward submarine warfare than were the Allies, particularly America.

Although German is not one of the pitifully few languages I can use, I eventually come up with the search term *Uunterseebootskrieg* and in an Ngram arrives at a page with quite similar graphs to our English language search found here. [5] [following page]

[4] Found at: http://www.google.com/search?q=%22submarine%20warfare%22&tbs=bks:1,cdr:1,cd_min:1800 ,cd_max:1917&lr=lang_en

[5] http://ngrams.googlelabs.com/graph?content=Unterseebootskrieg&year_start=1800&year_end=2000&corpus=8&smoothing=3 (Note: The capitalization of the 'U' in "Unterseebootskrieg" is important when performing an ngram search)

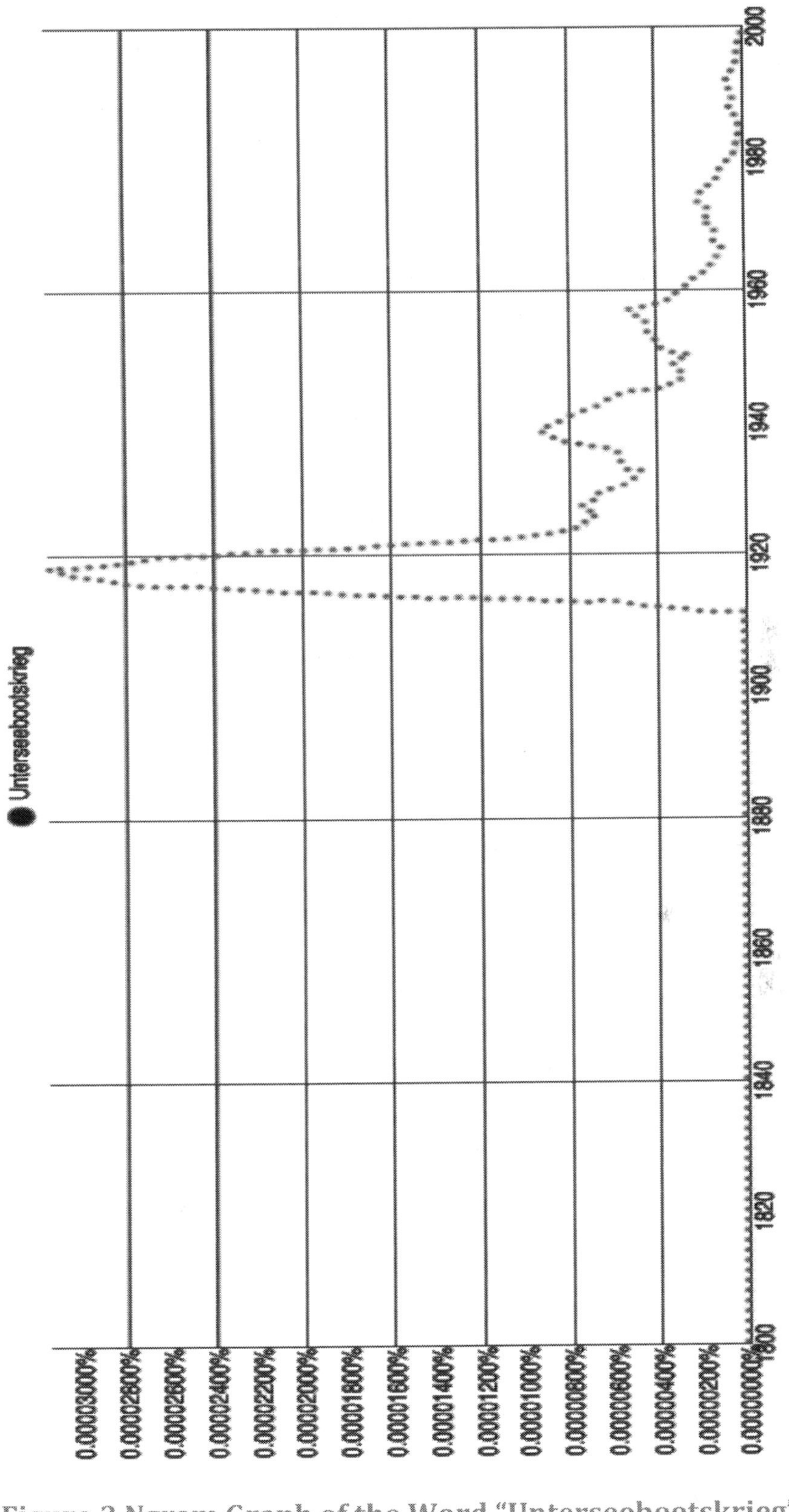

Figure 3 Ngram Graph of the Word "Unterseebootskrieg"

There are useful starts for our search, but we still need to see if the terms *submarine* and *criminal* are often linked in the periods we are studying. We arrive at this graph: [6] [following page]

[6] http://ngrams.googlelabs.com/graph?content=submarine%2C+criminal&year_start=1800&year_end=2000&corpus=0&smoothing=3

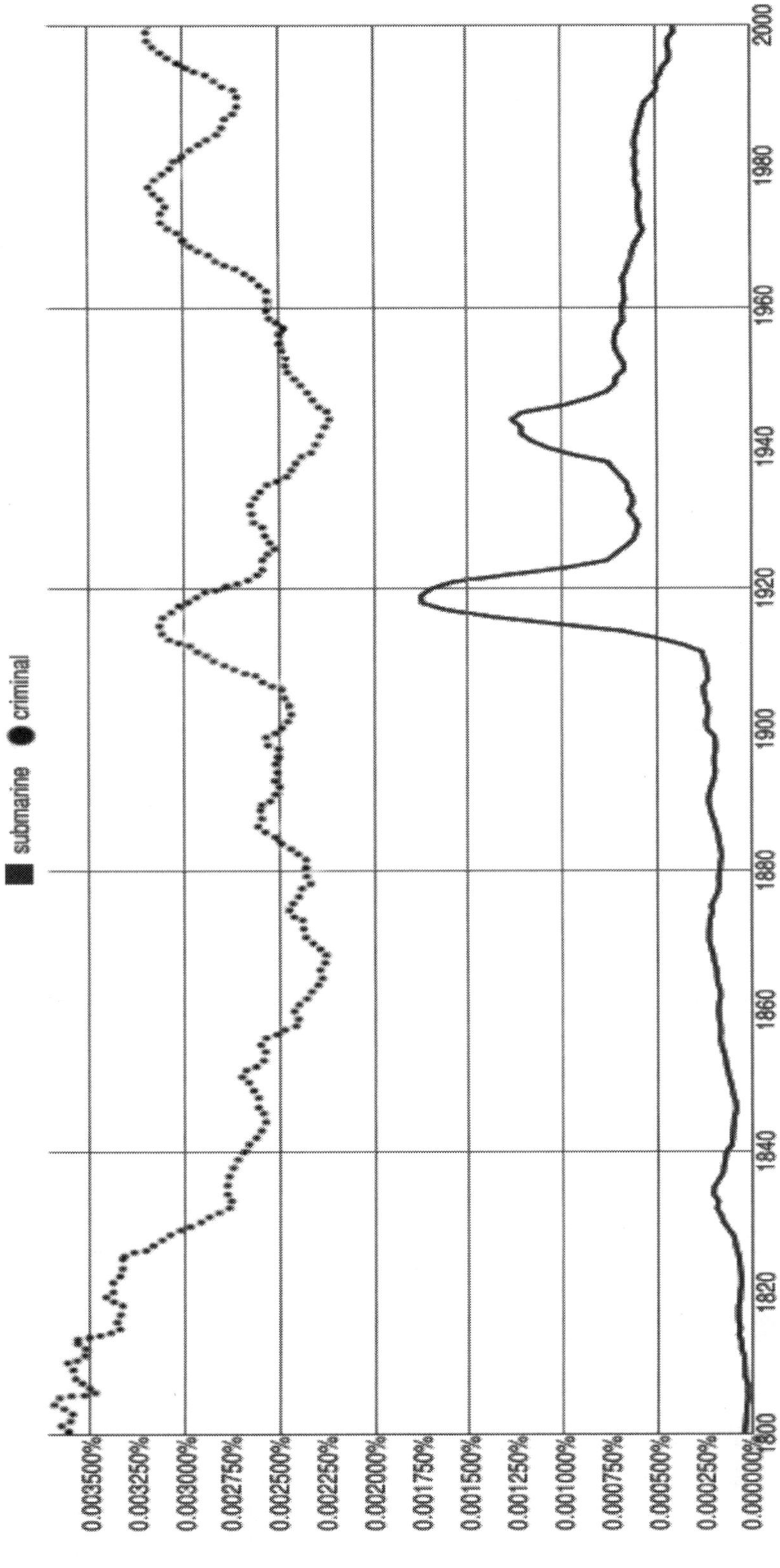

Figure 4 Ngram Graph of the Word "submarine" and "criminal"

Here we begin to learn a bit more. One of the student's assumptions seems to be holding up rather well. In English at least, the submarine seems to be less linked with the notion of "criminal" in the Second World War than in the First.

This is by no means a safe conclusion without much additional research, but it has shown some of the power of the Ngram viewer, and in addition our searches have led us to a number of useful sources.

There are some systematic issues of which users attempting major generalizations should be aware. There is an amusing analysis of the occurrence of the F word---or is it the S word? ---found here.[7] [4] However, there are also some distinct limitations in the device.[8] [5] Changes in spelling over time can be critical, and it is also difficult to be fully confident with the thoroughness of any given search.

We think that Ngram is a very powerful search tool and that it should be investigated by any one interested in changes in words or concepts over time. For those wishing to do high-level searches, Google permits the user to download discrete data sets and to manipulate them locally. So, like any Internet search, Ngram is only a beginning. It is also a great deal of fun. Once again, thanks, Google!

---

[7] http://searchengineland.com/when-ocr-goes-bad-googles-ngram-viewer-the-f-word-59181?utm_source=feedburner&utm_medium=feed&utm_campaign=Feed%3A+searchengineland+%28Search+Engine+Land%3A+Google%2C+Bing%2C+SEO%2C+PPC%2C+SEM+%26+Search+Marketing+ News%29

[8] For somewhat contrarian views go to: http://nataliacecire.blogspot.com/2010/12/google-books-ngrams-and-number-of-words. html

Peaceful Evolution in China and the World Wide Web. Part IV: The Internet as the Bulwark of Chinese Democracy?

By Jeffrey Barlow

Table of Contents

Introduction	**183**
The Presidential Succession	**184**
The Succession to Premier	**185**
Chinese Democracy?	**186**
The Internet and the Future of Chinese Democracy	**188**
Conclusion	**190**

Introduction

This is the fourth and concluding editorial in a series, "Peaceful Evolution in China and the World Wide Web". [1] To summarize the arguments thus far:

1. I have argued that a system with stable political factions functions very much like a system with two or more political parties, usually thought to be a critical element of a democratic political system, though not the only one.
2. In the Chinese system, consistent factions have been visible over recent years. At present, there are two important ones. First is the *Tuanpai*, a group associated with past leadership in the Chinese Youth League, the most dominant of Chinese mass organizations.
3. The second recognizable faction is the Princeling's faction. This is less well organized than the Tuanpai. It is formed not of those who have come up via a common political path, such as leadership in the Youth League, but of those who have descended from politically powerful or wealthy families.

---

[1] Jeffrey Barlow, "Peaceful Evolution in China and the World Wide Web: Part I, Two Democracies?" at: http://bcis.pacificu.edu/journal/article.php?id=98 and Jeffrey Barlow, "Peaceful Evolution in China and the World Wide Web: Part II, Factionalism and Democracy" at: http://bcis.pacificu.edu/journal/article.php?id=108 Part III is Peaceful Evolution in China and the World Wide Web: Part III, China's Emerging Leadership, at: http://bcis.pacificu.edu/journal/article.php?id=751

4. In the Chinese political system, both contemporary and historical, the most useful weapon wielded by factions was to charge that an opponent had violated core agreements on values, usually through personal corruption.

In this fourth and concluding article, we examine the probable successors to the two most important posts in China, the Presidency, now held by Hu Jintao, and the Premiership, now held by Wen JIaobao. We argue here that important changes are occurring in China, and that due in large part to the Internet as a conduit for Chinese popular voices, democratic interests will be much strengthened in this new era.

The Presidential Succession

Chinese leaders usually gain experience and reputation by proceeding through the bureaucratic structure, gaining experience first at local levels, then higher posts, usually heading up a province and often being entrusted with particularly sticky problems or ambitious plans. This has been the pattern for all major leaders since the death of Deng Xiaoping. As a result, the pool of probable successors to the two key posts, President and Premier, have been identifiable for some time. As the time to appoint new leaders will be during the meeting of the People's Consultative Congress in 2012, the front-runners become more apparent. [2]

We begin with the Presidency as it is widely recognized as the more important of the two offices, and thought to be the top position for which a Chinese political figure can aspire. This position evolved from the all-powerful Party Chairmanship of Mao Zedong. It is currently a position elected by the largest of China's legislative bodies, the People's Consultative Congress, composed of elected officials who have risen through a narrow electoral process, which in a broad sense is dominated by the Chinese Communist Party (CCP). Its decisions are clearly often the result of factional politics. It has at times overridden the Party in important matters; at other times it has been reminded of its subordinate position to the Party. Hu Jintao now serves as both head of state (President) and as head (General Secretary) of the Chinese Communist Party.

Most analysts assume at present that Xi Jinping, a member of the emerging younger generation of leaders, will succeed Hu Jintao, the current President, though this is by no means inevitable. [3] The reasons usually given for this

---

[2] Note that we focus upon two such leaders here. However, there is a pool of at least 6 such leaders, any one of which could be considered qualified potential candidates.

[3] The New York Times, in "China Grooming Deft Politician as Next Leader" by EDWARD WONG and JONATHAN ANSFIELD January 23, 2011, refers to this succession as a result of China

assumption revolve around the fact that Xi Jinping is clearly close to Hu, has been given ever-greater responsibilities and introduced on important world stages over the last year or so. It is also held to be in his favor and that he has good connections in the army, having served in a number of military posts. These indications, while suggestive, might be said to obscure the fact that, above all, Xi Jinping is a very competent individual with considerable experience, education, and expertise in fields associated with economic growth and development. [4] It is no longer enough for a political figure to rise to power through CCP politics alone.

Xi Jinping is widely regarded as a member of the Princeling faction because his father, Xi Zhongxun, was a Deputy Premier and once the Governor of Guangdong province. Zhongxun was reportedly purged for criticizing the government for its handling of the events at Tiananmen in 1989. This makes Xi Jinping particularly interesting to Western analysts, always seeking some fissure in the Chinese leadership.

The Succession to Premier

Another very powerful position is that of Premier. This was formerly the position of Zhou Enlai in the early days of the government of the Peoples' Republic (PRC) following 1949. He was widely regarded as the more popular and accessible right hand of the dictatorial Chairman Mao. The Premier also serves at the will of the National People's Congress, and like the President/Chairman, is subservient to the Central Committee of the Chinese Communist Party. Each of these posts is selected every five years and each can serve for only two terms or ten years.

This position is quite powerful and more deeply rooted in the Chinese civil bureaucracy than is the Presidency as such, though the Presidency is usually regarded as the more powerful of the two positions. The current Premier is Wen Jiaobao.

The fact that Wen Jiaobao is a member of the Tuanpai faction is important. He came up through the most broadly based of Chinese political groups and is responsible for the office with the broadest influence in the bureaucracy. During

---

"Following a secretive succession plan sketched out years ago" at:
http://www.nytimes.com/2011/01/24/world/asia/24leader.html
This is, in my opinion, nonsense. The succession was a result of a long-term process wherein a number of strong leaders came to the top of the political process in a process which consisted largely of showing their abilities to accomplish important tasks. As stated above there at least six such potential candidates, though there may be frontrunners as in any political transition.

[4] A very well sourced Wikipedia article is found at: http://en.wikipedia.org/wiki/Xi_Jinping

the Cultural Revolution for example, Zhou Enlai was often credited for protecting the bureaucracy from the excesses of extreme Leftists, who were often urged on by Mao himself.

Li Keqiang, it is widely believed, will succeed Wen Jiaobao. Like Wen Jiaobao, Li Keqiang came up through the Youth League and is thus a member of the Tuanpai faction. He has unusual credentials: a law (LLB) degree from Beijing University and a Ph.D. in economics. He has spent a great deal of time in, not only, organizational work, but also in the management of the Chinese economy. He has represented China at the highest-ranking international economic organizations, including at the Davos World Economic Forum in 2010. [5] Like Xi Jinping, then, he has been introduced to the world over several years.

Li Keqiang, like Xi Jinping, is committed to reform in China, and is exceptionally experienced, well educated, and also like Xi Jinping, has specialized in issues dealing with growth and development. Neither of these individuals is by any means a stereotypical Communist Chinese leader; both are extremely competent and well qualified for either of the two highest offices. Li Keqiang is usually thought to be much more engaged in social reform than is Xi Jinping.

Chinese Democracy?

Although I have chosen to follow the conventional wisdom in assuming here that Xi Jinping will become President, succeeding Hu Jintao, and Li Keqiang Premier, succeeding Wen Jiaobao, in fact either man is clearly well qualified for either office. These forecasts depend in large part upon the fact that the Chinese political system is factionalized. Xi Jinping is closely associated with Hu Jintao, and Li Keqiang seems to be following smoothly in the train of Wen Jiaobao, the current leader of the Tuanpai.

These factions do not constitute major fissures in the Chinese leadership. Individuals commonly cross over factional lines. Hu Jintao, for example, who is apparently favoring the Princeling Xi Jinping as his successor, is usually thought of as a member of the Tuanpai as well as is the Premier, Wen Jiaobao. It is the process of interaction between these two factions that should interest us.

---

[5] See his performance at Davos on You Tube
at: http://www.youtube.com/watch?v=ybzXrKw6rPk
He began there by quoting Confucius before Marx or Mao, if he ever did quote them. For a variety of very reformist positions taken by Li see http://en.wikipedia.org/wiki/Li_Keqiang. Though this is a Wikipedia article and based in Chinese sources, its content agrees with widely published reports and I find it satisfactory.

There is still a year or more before the selection process will be finalized, and either man would remain loyal to the system, is unlikely to scream that the other is a traitor or a secret capitalist, or to imply darkly that violent action would be an appropriate response to an unexpected twist in history.

Of the two men, Xi Jinping is the more frangible candidate. As a Princeling, his selection somewhat violates the usual expectation that all Chinese leaders will be "men of the people" and there is certainly a deep suspicion on the part of many Chinese of those who "take a helicopter" ---rise suddenly and unexpectedly---or who "walk through the back door"---use personal connections to attain a goal. Xi Jinping, however, presided over a political house cleaning in notoriously corrupt Shanghai, demonstrating his ability to get tough with power, and is a noted nationalist who has lectured foreigners on the error of their ways in criticizing China. Like Li Keqiang, he was "sent down" during the Cultural Revolution to work in the countryside.

It is certainly possible to see a political system that has produced two such qualified leaders as a successful one. But is it democratic? Not in the American sense of being the result of an electoral process dominated by two parties who produced candidates who regularly have undergone competitions at the ballot box. [6]

However, they did come up through mass organizations at which leadership was chosen through electoral processes, albeit restricted ones. If they were not in that sense popular, they would not be where they are today. [7]

---

[6] I will forego any of the many qualifications that this description of an ideal American political process brings to my own cynical mind. Provide your own.

[7] It should be noted that there is a troublesome drawback to widespread electoral democracy in China. Where elections are held, local figures almost always win them. This is the same group which is largely responsible for local corruption. It is the central government which prosecutes corruption, and yet outsiders to a local area, who would have more interest in supporting central government policies, because posted into that area by the central government, will rarely win such elections.

The Internet and the Future of Chinese Democracy

The Internet has acquired a steadily increasing influence upon the Chinese political system. We often make a great deal of Chinese attempts to block information. However, Chinese who care can quickly learn how to evade such censorship and quickly acquire the necessary means to do so. Chinese who do not do so are unusually loyal, particularly timid, or more often, simply apathetic.[8]

The coming era of new leadership further increases the leverage of Chinese public opinion. Local abuses of power or conspicuous examples of corruption have been the subject of many Internet campaigns over the past several years.

Charges or corruption or abuse of power not only quickly go viral on the internal Chinese net, but also international once they reach a certain level of impact domestically.[9] The Internet also serves to advance factional political positions, especially the common and very serious charge that a leader is abusing his power for personal gain.

Such factional issues and divisions will also have the inevitable consequence of furthering another element of democracy currently being strengthened in China, the rule of law. Abuses of power and corruption are already illegal in China, but the laws are inadequately enforced and too often political influence allows miscreants to avoid prosecution. Once corruption becomes a political issue, however, it too will easily become a wedge issue between the factions.
It is noteworthy that both Li Keqiang and Xi Jinping have studied law in formal contexts. Li Keqiang studied in Beijing University's Faculty of Law as an undergraduate; Xi Jingping holds a doctoral degree in law.[10]

There is one overriding question: will Li Keqiang, as Premier, and as leader of the Tuanpai faction, serve to push forward the process of social reforms such as strengthening health care, workers rights, and social security in China? Will he consistently advocate democracy and rule of law in China? There are several reasons to expect that Li Keqiang will also do so. An important one is that it is in

---

[8] I recognize, of course, that well-known dissidents often are punished or intimidated for being notorious and consistent opponents of the government. This is, however, a separate issue, I believe, from the question of whether or not there are competing factions within the leadership.

[9] An excellent example is the trope now being used to shame abuses of power, "My Father is Li Gang!" To fully understand this issue with all its relationships to the criticism of abuse of power via the Internet, go to: http://globalvoicesonline.org/2010/10/22/china-my-father-is-li-gang/

[10] http://www.chinatoday.com/who/x/xi-jinping.htm It should be noted that many Ph.D, degrees held by Chinese political figures were attained through part-time study and are widely regarded as not equivalent to a full-time degree, whether Chinese or Western.

the interests of the Tuanpai to do so. Here is, reprinted, a paragraph from a previous editorial:

> *"The Tuanpai might be said to be the most broadly representative of Chinese factions in that the Youth League is the largest of the mass organizations which combine to shape the CPC. It is also the organization with the closest ties to grass roots groups as it is present at every level where large numbers of youth are found, including all educational institutions, reaching right down to the lower grades if we count the groups of younger students organized by the League. It is also found among peasant and labor organizations, among women's and other special interest groups."*

The Tuanpai or Youth League, then, is the most broadly representative of all the mass membership organizations that feed into the CPC. It will most directly reflect the opinion of the bureaucracy and of many leadership types distributed throughout Chinese society.

Another reason to believe that Li Keqiang will be active in supporting reform is that recent leaders who have come out of the Tuanpai are often associated with pressures for reform toward a Chinese version of democracy. These include Hu Yaobang, former General Secretary of the CPC, who was removed by Deng Xiaoping, because of Hu's attempt to protect student protestors prior to Tiananmen; current Premier Wen JIaobao, and current President Hu Jintao.

If prognostications of the succession are correct, and the Princeling Xi Jingping is elected President, and the Tuanpai faction member Li Keqiang becomes Premier, then the Tuanpai might be regarded as having been relegated to a secondary role in the upcoming transition. The Tuanpai has both Presidency and Premiership in the current government. This relative demotion could be an indication that the CPC itself is uneasy at recent moves toward a more open society in China.

Indications are, however, that the Tuanpai heritage and its ties to Chinese style grassroots democracy will continue. At the time of this writing (January 2011), Premier Wen Jiaobao "...appeared at the nation's top petition bureau in Beijing, where people go to file grievances, and encouraged citizens to criticize the government and press their cases for justice." The visit was widely reported in China, and thousands of postings approving of the visit quickly appeared on the Internet. [11]

---

[11] DAVID BARBOZA "China Leader Encourages Criticism of Government" The New York Times, Januray 26,2011.
http://www.nytimes.com/2011/01/27/world/asia/27china.html?scp=1&sq=Barboza%20China%20leader&st=cse

Assuming that Xi Jinping is chosen as President, as a Princeling, he will be particularly vulnerable to grassroots campaigns because he is a member of the Princeling faction. Charges that the President is not dealing with what is widely recognized as the most serious problem facing China, corruption among officials at local levels, would acquire new resonance while a Princeling is the head of government.

Another wild card in this process is the National People's Congress (NPC) itself. It is widely regarded as a rubber stamp for the CPC, but in recent years it has asserted increasing autonomy. Even the CPC Party Congress, which will meet prior to the NPC, has often failed to elect Princelings to its key governing bodies, perhaps out of a populist antagonism to such leaders. [12]

Conclusion

It is important to understand what I am not saying here. There is a consistent trope in the American press and amongst many citizens that regimes regarded as oppressive over the world, are continually on the verge of an overthrow and presumably, would move toward an American democratic model. This hope in part fueled American actions in Iraq and is always in the background of our attitudes toward Iran. At present, we are making comfortable assumptions about political turmoil in Egypt and Yemen which implicitly place them into such a context.

China is not such a case. All indications, and certainly my personal experience in living and working in China a month or more each year for the past six years, suggest that the great majority of Chinese people are unusually content and comfortable with their government and their political system. Its economic progress has made it the envy of the world.

Certainly China has, like every rapidly changing social system, many problems crying out for better solutions. This is particularly true of relations between majority Han and ethnic minorities, and in relations between the central government and minority political regions, especially Tibet and Muslim areas. Certainly many Chinese people hope to see even faster progress, but China is far from violent outbreaks that might threaten the system itself.

Therefore, I am not arguing that factional politics will overthrow the Communist Party of China and usher in a new age dominated by American style democracy. Rather, I believe, factional politics, bolstered by electronic communications, will inevitably cause the Communist Party itself, and the state, to advance the cause

---

[12] Or so Cheng Li speculates. Cheng Li, "China's Fifth Generation: Is Diversity a Source of Strength or Weakness?" Pg. 84-5 at: http://www.nbr.org/publications/element.aspx?id=147

of Chinese democracy, eventually producing another interesting variant among the many international versions of democracy.

As Americans, we may choose to ignore this process, to compare it unfavorably to our own very troubled and dysfunctional democracy, but other democracies will not care much about that. Neither should they.

Studying China Online: Editorial Review

Editorial By Jeffrey Barlow

Introduction

The amount of information discussing China now found online has grown considerably over the last several decades. While we hope that this growth is creating a proportionately greater understanding of China, this does not necessarily follow. Understanding China has long been a serious challenge for Westerners in general and for Americans in particular.

China has often been for the West the "Other"—viewed not so much for what it truly is, but rather as that which we ourselves are not. China is often presented simply as a cautionary example: "Sure, China has great economic growth, unlike the U.S. recently, but China does not have freedom of religion, so there is nothing to be learned from it!" is the sort of twisted trope that is often encountered.

This function of China as the "other" has been supported by a systematic set of stereotypes about Asia, often termed "Orientalism." [1] Orientalism presents Asia, including China, in terms that in the past functioned to justify Western dominance as appropriate and necessary because China was afflicted with an entire constellation of negative characteristics such as backwardness, incompetence, and corruption. Obviously, if these attributions were ever justified, they are no longer appropriate in this era of rapid increases in Chinese economic strength.

The fact that it has long been difficult to understand China, however, is not to say that it is impossible. Materials dealing with China are now more easily available than ever before, many of which can be found online.

In this editorial we consider first the issue of the quantity of materials concerning China now available and their quality. We conclude by introducing WWW sites and materials that the reader may find useful in constructing his or her own understanding of China.

---

[1] A very good discussion of Edward Said, the name most associated with the notion of Orientalism, from his book by that same name, can be found at: http://en.wikipedia.org/wiki/Orientalism_%28book%29

Is there now more information on China?

To test our belief that much more information is now available on China, we relied primarily on a search of the digital materials published by *The New York Times*, simply because we have regularly used it for our own research (and hence understand its layout and general approach to the news) and because its search functions permit considerable variation on search terms and on the time period searched. [2]

This is not an ideal or exhaustive search, because we know that the news space in the NYT, as extensive as it is relative to other newspapers, is in fact limited relative to ad space, etc. Only a small fraction of potential news and information about China can appear in the NYT. However, even this basic and limited tool is very useful.

To begin, we first ran a simple search on the occurrence of the term "China" in the NYT over the past several decades:

By decades:

- From 1/1981-12/1990 there were total 19,773 occurrences of articles in which the word "China" appeared.
- From 1/1991-12/2000 there were 24,728 occurrences.
- From 1/1/2001-12/31/2010 there were 45,800 occurrences.

These numbers suggest more than a doubling from 1981-1990 to 2001-10; by far the biggest increase came during the decade 2001-2010. From this it is easy to conclude that yes, there is much more information available about China than was the case in the past several decades, and that the amount may be increasing rapidly at present.

Just as an indication of the total volume of material on China vis-à-vis our own sample, let's compare the NYT production of digital material on China during 2010 to that of the Internet as a whole as indicated by a Google search. The NYT had 5800 references (primarily in article headings) to China over the past year. The same search ("China", past year) turns up 3,580,000,000 English language Internet pages with the same word. So the NYT China-related content is a very small fraction of the total. While we have not demonstrated this, it also seems

---

[2] This sort of content search might seem a very impressionistic and uncertain means of assessing public concerns, but it is a time-honored methodology in scholarship and often yields very interesting and useful results; we believe it does so here. In Chinese Studies, see such works as Harold Roberts Isaacs, Scratches on our minds: American images of China and India (1958), and the many works of Richard W. Steele. See also the Pew databases at: http://pewglobal.org/database/?indicator=24&survey=6&response=Favorable&mode=chart

reasonable to assume that the total content on the Internet has also grown substantially over the past several decades.

Now that we have demonstrated that yes, there is more information available on China than ever before (at least in the NYT) let us now see what might be useful to a concerned student of China. What are the various ways of using the WWW to increase our understanding?

Our methodology here is again a very simple one; we are listing materials with which we are personally familiar, or those which have been recommended by professionals in the field, most often by Clare Richardson-Barlow and her friends from the graduate programs at the Monterey Institute of International Studies or at Tsinghua University in Beijing.

We have broken the resources discussed here into categories below. However, these categories are somewhat artificial. Many sites incorporate a wide variety of media, including text, video, blogs, commenting systems, etc.

News Sites

The New York Times: http://www.nytimes.com/ The NYT is, unfortunately, currently groping for a business model that might enable it to benefit from its status as "America's Newspaper of Record." This includes, sadly, charging for digital access. But a registered reader can still get a number of free stories per month. Nonetheless, the NYT remains the single largest source of material on China. [3] In following the NYT, however, some stories seem to me to be more balanced than others. Some have argued that the NYT sometimes "frames" China stories in a manner that places news events in contexts which are themselves political, even when discussing seemingly apolitical events such as SARS, flood or earthquake relief, etc. [4] Always read any material from any source with a very critical perspective. If the information is important to you, then be sure to get differing views.

---

[3] For evidence of the importance of the NYT see: Jonathan Stray, "The Google/China hacking case: How many news outlets do the original reporting on a big story?" Neiman Journalism Lab, February 24, 2010.

[4] See, for example, first the NYT story at: http://www.nytimes.com/2008/04/29/world/americas/29iht-students.1.12424235.html
Then see the blog commentary at:http://omnologos.wordpress.com/2008/04/30/evidence-of-anti-china-reporting-bias-in-the-ihtnyt.
See also http://www.overcomingbias.com/2010/01/china-bashing.html.
See especially this M.A. thesis: Ning SongThe Framing of China's Bird Flu Epidemic by U.S. Newspapers Influencial in China: How the New York Times and The Washington Post Linked the Image of the Nation to the Handling of the Disease Full text available in PDF download at:
http://digitalarchive.gsu.edu/communication_theses/27/

The Wall Street Journal: http://online.wsj.com/home-page By digital subscription. Currently $2.00 per week plus one free month; see especially The **ChinaRealTimeReport** at: http://blogs.wsj.com/chinarealtime/.

The Economist: http://www.economist.com/ A major source on economic and political news. It is highly regarded and very free market oriented. Seemingly free, though many special reports are not. http://www.economist.com/node/18709581

Financial Times: http://www.ft.com/world/asiapacific/china Free registration for limited use. A wide variety of economic news.

Bloomberg: http://www.bloomberg.com/ is a leading source of business and economics news. Bloomberg maintains its own research and reporting bureau. I find the site very pragmatic with good analysis. Free iPhone app available as well. Free access. My own first choice for business news with an international flavor.

Huffington Post: http://www.huffingtonpost.com/ A major source of digital news and opinions. It frequently leads major stories before they hit print. Free; run searches on China, Taiwan, etc.,

NBR Reports: http://www.pbs.org/nbr/ National Public Broadcasting's Nightly Business Reports on line. Podcasts and Twitter links, Facebook.

The Epoch Times: http://www.theepochtimes.com/ This is the newspaper of the Fa Lun Gong movement, a banned group in China. To most Americans, this is an issue of religious freedom. To the Chinese government, the organization is a dangerous cult. To me, it is both the above and also a typical millenarian Buddhist pyramid scam. For the most critical views of China, go here.

English-language newspapers with strong Chinese views from "Greater China" which includes Hong Kong, Singapore, and Chinese communities overseas such as Malaysia, etc.

The China Daily: http://www.chinadaily.com.cn/index.html The China Daily is closely controlled by the CPC (Chinese Communist Party) and is clearly a subjective source. For those of us who have been reading such Chinese sources for many years (Since 1965 in my particular case). it is much more open, and readable than such Chinese sources have ever been. It is most useful as a sort of gauge as to how the Chinese are responding to issues, both international and internal to China. It is also useful for the close student of China to always ask the question, "Now how could the Chinese possibly come to these conclusions…?" The China Daily has interactive sections where you can read comments by Chinese (and foreign readers) on the news and even post your own views. http://www.chinadaily.com.cn/opinion/2011-05/20/content_12550029.htm

The China Economic Review: http://newcer.chinaeconomicreview.com/ began in the United Kingdom and then was purchased by Hong Kong and Chinese interests. It draws on a large number of Western perspectives and is usually thought of as relatively independent in its views.

China Today: http://www.chinatoday.com/ Chinese portal to many English language sources; it also aggregates materials on China from Western sources.

April Media: http://en.m4.cn/ is a very interesting, clearly and strongly nationalist media site operated by a graduate of Beijing's prestigious Tsinghua University. It is provocative and opinionated. Read it!
http://en.m4.cn/archives/9136.html

South China Morning Post: . Out of Hong Kong, the SCMP is one of the most reliable voices on Greater China, which includes China, Taiwan, Hong Kong and Singapore and other overseas Chinese communities. See it at:
http://www.scmp.com/portal/site/SCMP/
(Iit carries a free 14-day trial after which it is about four U.S. dollars per month.)

Xinhua: http://www.xinhuanet.com/english2010/ Xinhua is another official Chinese English-language source. Again, when reading it, you must understand that it is both an official Chinese source and simultaneously a useful window into Chinese opinions.
Sino Daily http://www.sinodaily.com/ has a variety of specialized sites dealing with agriculture, space technology, with Chinese and Western points of view.

Sino Daily: http://www.sinodaily.com/ has a variety of specialized sites dealing with agriculture, space technology, with Chinese and Western points of view.

News Aggregators:

These are sites that collect links to stories appearing other places. Sometimes these are "pushed" to your desktop, other times, you go to them as useful portal sites.

Asia Chronicle: http://asianchronicle.com/ It aggregates news dealing with Asia. The World News (WN) Network was founded in 1995 and launched online in 1998, with the primary objective of being the most comprehensive, one-stop news resource on the Internet. Today, World News has over 20,000 global thematic and regional news sites.

UN Wire: http://www.unfoundation.org/our-solutions/campaigns/un-wire/ A daily email digest of issues facing the U.N. It is free and can be targeted to your particular interests. It aggregates news stories from the international press.

Hacker News: http://news.ycombinator.com/news An aggregator of news impacting hi-tech.

More Specialized Periodicals such as scholarly journals and research reports:

Brookings: http://www.brookings.edu/ A variety of free materials from a major non-profit. http:/www.brookings.edu/china.aspx

US Chamber of Commerce:
http://www.uschamber.com/international/asia/china Views of U.S. businesses in China. Free reports from a business perspective.
http://www.uschamber.com/international/asia/china/china-policy-resources

Stratfor: at http://www.stratfor.com/ This is an independent think tank which delivers daily updates with an emphasis upon milatry, economic, and political developments. There is a free one week access which would let you decide if this is a useful investment for you. http://www.stratfor.com/stratfor_search?s=china

Asia Society: http://asiasociety.org/ A Non-profit Center in New York. Neo-Liberal point of view on China.

Devex: http://www.devex.com/en/ An international development group; the site has a good job search and resume posting. It is also a networking site and is free.

Eurasia Group: http://www.eurasiagroup.net/ It treats business and politics as linked. Many free reports and daily stories from the world press, more services for paying clients

Foreign Affairs: http://www.foreignaffairs.com/ The leading liberal journal on foreign affairs with limited access for major pieces, but lots of interesting short notices. Digital subscription is $32.00 per year and includes 50 years of archives.

The McKinsey Quarterly: https://www.mckinseyquarterly.com/
A research group, which does wonderful brief reports. See for example, on Chinese Internet Users: https://www.mckinseyquarterly.com /Segmenting_Chinas_digital_consumers_2795

NWCC The Northwest China Council:, which sponsors many events in the Pacific Northwest and has many resources available to members is found at: Organization that sponsors many events in the Pacific Northwest and has many resources available to members, is found at: http://www.nwchina.org/

Pew Research Center: http://pewresearch.org/ You may not find this site useful very often, but when it is useful, it can be very useful indeed, as it does constant opinion sampling on a wide variety of topics. We use it quite frequently. You will find years of specialized reports free and downloadable as PDFs.

World Politics Review: http://www.worldpoliticsreview.com/ or http://about.worldpoliticsreview.com/overview/ A very broad site with a great deal of Asian information and daily newsletters for media stories you can sign up to receive. See for example this aggregation of new stories focusing on cyberspace in Asia: http://www.worldpoliticsreview.com/issues/14/media-and-communications Free trial or 99 USD annually

Wiley-Blackwell: http://www.wiley.com/WileyCDA/Brand/id-35.html Major publishing house with a great catalogue with specialized titles dealing with China and many other topics.

Blogs

Note —Many "Chinese" blogs are written by foreigners living in China, "expats" or expatriates. Sometimes these are insightful and useful; often they are cynical, even hostile and very snarky.

ChinaSmack: http://www.chinasmack.com/ is a media portal that focuses on Internet-related issues and pop culture in China. It is often "R" rated and the layout is rather chaotic, but it has excellent archives and searches can often turn up surprising perspectives of Chinese Netizens. See, for example, the discussion on the death of Bin Laden, found at: http://www.chinasmack.com/2011/stories/osama-bin-laden-dead-chinese-netizen-reactions.html

The Peking Duck: http://www.pekingduck.org/ While I am not too familiar with this one, I liked its broad coverage and apparent objectivity.

China Blog List: Http://www.chinabloglist.org/ for an extensive list of English-language blogs written (usually) by English speaking expatriates. Want to know what they think about any given topic? Ask them!

Cryptogram Bruce Schneier: http://www.schneier.com/crypto-gram.html Blogs and emails dealing with security issues, particularly cybersecuriity. Good, even analysis.

Twitter Sites

Like all Twitter feeds, you may find these mindlessly irrelevant or exactly what interests you...

Sinofinance: http://twitter.com/#!/sinofinance twitter feeds.

The Sino Gglance Twitter: http://twitter.com/#!/thesinoglance

DTN Asia Twitter: http://twitter.com/#!/DTNAsia

DigitalFellows Twitter: http://twitter.com/#!/wisat/digitalfellows Twitter feed re digital content business from technology to consumer behavior.

Learning Chinese Online

The Oregon Virtual Education Center has created a site for teaching Chinese language on line. This will be the first run of the class, go to the above site to learn more. http://www.orved.org/content/chinese-language-classes-start-fall

Mandarin tools — Twitter and web resource http://www.mandarintools.com/ A very comprehensive site for learning Chinese on line. Some very sophisticated tools for all levels and all purposes. The Chinese dictionary and flash card training program (for smart phones) comes highly recommended. Trial account.

http://www.chinese-tools.com/learn/chinese A useful site, apparently totally free for introductory lessons.

http://www.trainchinese.com/v1/a_user/index.php Train Chinese: for smart phones, great dictionary and flash card program- must pay for upgrade.

A nice site: http://www.aaronpinero.com/mandarin/learning/34-apps/60-dianhua-dicitonary discusses online dictionaries and advanced use of the iPhone for studying Chinese.

http://www.appolicious.com/curated-apps/172-best-mandarin-chinese-learning-apps This is also a nice site for iPhone users.

Chinese Learn Online at: http://www.chineselearnonline.com/ver1/ I have no experience with this site, but I am impressed by the apparent ease of use and think the podcasts an excellent tool. It has a number of free lessons available so you should be able to try it and make your own decision as to whether or not it works for you.

Cyberwar and China

Interface: http://bcis.pacificu.edu/journal/ In the e-journal Interface of the Berglund Center for Internet Studies, which I edit, I often review works concerning cyberwar issues or write about them myself. See http://bcis.pacificu.edu/journal/search.php and run searches cyberwar and cyber war.

Conclusion

We hope that our audience will find the materials and sites discussed here useful. It is very important to remember, however, one of the grave dangers of Internet research: it is all too easy to confine oneself to a university of data and opinions about which we are very positive because they agree with our existing prejudices. It is very important to read a wide variety of opinions and of resources lest we become like the frog living in a well described by Mao Zedong: "He thinks the sky is only as big as the top of the well. If he surfaced, he would have an entirely different view." [5] All serious students of China must try continually to examine the wider sky of opinions, both Chinese and American.

---

[5] http://thinkexist.com/quotation/we_think_too_small-like_the_frog_at_the_bottom_of/153576.html

About the Authors

Jeffrey G. Barlow, Ph.D.

Jeffrey Barlow has been the Director of the Berglund Center from 2000-2011. He is the founding editor of several peer-reviewed scholarly e-journals, including the Journal of History and Computing, now housed at the University of Michigan and E-AsPac, the e-journal of the Association for Asian Studies on the Pacific Coast. He has given invited lectures in the U.S., Canada, and China on topics related to the Internet.

Jeffrey's academic training at the University of California, Berkeley, was in Modern Chinese History. He is also a recognized authority on Chinese immigration into the Pacific Northwest, and on Chinese use of the Internet. He taught at the University of Oregon and at Lewis and Clark College before coming to Pacific in 1994. He has worked with the Berglund Center since its beginnings. Jeffrey has since retired from his position as Director of the Berglund Center and as a professor of history at Pacific University.

Jeff Cain, Ed.D., MS

Jeff Cain, EdD, MS, is an Adjunct Associate Professor in the Department of Pharmacy Practice & Science and the Director of Education Technology at the University of Kentucky College of Pharmacy. He received his EdD in Instruction and Administration, his MS in Instructional Design, and a BBA in finance from the University of Kentucky. In addition to co-directing and teaching a pharmacy management course, he is actively involved in social and educational research. His primary research interests are social media, e-professionalism, Web 2.0 applications in education and health science professions, and educational technology. Dr. Cain's diverse professional background includes work as an engineer for OshKosh B'Gosh, Inc. and owning/managing a small landscaping business. He has worked in the fields of higher education and technology since 1999 and has numerous publications and presentations pertaining to Web 2.0, social media, teaching and learning, and instructional technology – particularly as they relate to the profession of pharmacy and pharmacy education. He is an active member of the American Association of Colleges of Pharmacy (AACP) and currently serves as an associate editor of *Currents in Pharmacy Teaching and Learning*.

Michael T. Charles, Ph.D., M.A

Dr. Mike Charles is an Associate Professor of Education at the College of Education at Pacific University. Dr. Mike Charles is an educational media and technology specialist with a background in curriculum and instruction. He taught in grades K-6 for 15 years in Phoenix, Arizona, working as a K-6 computer resource teacher for the final six years. His research interests include the way that technology enables student-initiated project learning environments, uses of visualization tools in teaching mathematics and science in K-12 education, and the complexities involved in changing teacher practice.

Elizabeth M. Drake-Boyt, Ph.D.

Dr. Drake-Boyt has provided continuous undergraduate distance learning courses in the Liberal Arts fields of Humanities, Theatre History/Appreciation, and Gender Studies for the University of Southern Indiana since 2008. As an adjunct, she taught one section of FYS for Pacific University in the Fall of 2010, and a Winter III 2011 Special Topics course intersecting humanities with performing arts. She has contracted with Portland Community College Community Education to provide a summer 2012 personal enrichment course: "The Extraordinarily Unknown". Her PhD was awarded with distinction by Florida State University in Humanities Interdisciplinary with Performing Arts in 2005. She has since published two books in dance history topics, and currently lives in Cherry Grove, OR. Articles written for *Interface* have been on the topic of practical issues and logistics required in effectively teaching entirely asynchronous online classes with the complexities of qualitative analysis required in a liberal arts Core Curriculum course.

Leonard D. DuBoff, JD

Leonard D. DuBoff is an attorney specializing in business and intellectual property law. Leonard was a professor of law at Northwestern School of Law of Lewis & Clark College for 23 years and has pioneered the field of art law, written extensively on the subject, and lectured all over the world on business and intellectual property. His two-volume text entitled The Deskbook of Art Law is frequently referred to by judges, lawyers, legal commentators and others who are interested in finding out about this important field of law, and it has also been adopted by several law schools as the basis for their courses on art law.

Christopher J. Ferguson, Ph.D.
Chris Ferguson is an associate professor of psychology at Texas A&M International University. He is a leading researcher of video games and youth behavior, recently serving as guest editor for the American Psychological Association journal Review of General Psychology's special issue on video games. He lives in Laredo, Texas with his wife and young son.

Jacob Fischer, Berglund Student Fellow
Jacob Fischer was a Freshman at Pacific University (2010-2011) with an interest in music and the Internet. Jacob was awarded the Berglund Student Fellowship Award during the 2010-2011 school year.

Michael Geraci, M.S.
Michael Geraci is an associate professor in Pacific University's Integrated Media program. Mike also teaches online courses for the University of Oregon's Applied Information Management Masters program, where he received his Master of Science degree in 2002. Prior to teaching, Mike spent eight years managing Pacific's department of Educational Technologies. In addition, he has experience working as an independent web developer, graphic designer and video production specialist. Mike's scholarly interests center upon the continued evolution of the Web, user experience, and typographic design.

Jamaica King, Berglund Student Fellow

Jamaica King is originally from the Mariana Islands, currently residing in Oregon. She is a Pacific University student majoring in Psychology and minoring in Computer Science. Jamaica is a 2010-2011 Berglund Student Fellow with interest in online gaming communities. She is passionate about video games and community satisfaction. Jamaica is currently in Southern California working for Riot Games as a Community Intern. Jamaica has written a great deal for *Interface* and has attended several gaming conferences, which were helpful in her attaining her dream job.

Christine Macfarlane, Ph.D.

Christine Macfarlane began her teaching career in the DOD schools as a general educator. After transitioning to special education, she taught students with severe, multiple disabilities for 5 years focusing on communication skills, problem behaviors, and assessment. In 1983, Chris joined USU as a clinical demonstration teacher, followed by co-directing federally funded grants and serving as a clinical instructor and research assistant professor. In 1991 Dr. Macfarlane became the Coordinator, Mental Disabilities Program, Department of Special Education, University of Northern Iowa. Chris arrived at Pacific University in August 2000 to develop and implement a special education program in collaboration with local school districts. An innovative internship program evolved, involving multiple school districts and several hundred-teacher candidates over the past 12 years. Over the years she has conducted research on the use of technology in teacher preparation, expert systems, and special education in Slovakia and China.

In addition, Chris has continued to work with parents, consult with school districts, and work internationally. In 1995 she provided technical assistance to the Department of Mental Retardation at Comenius University in Bratislava, Slovakia as part of a USAID grant. While there, she worked with faculty, students, and parents of children with disabilities. In 2006/07 she returned to Slovakia to document changes. Most recently, Chris joined faculty and students in a service project to Chongqing Province, China in July 2011 to provide training and support to a pediatric rehabilitation hospital in Chongqing and an orphanage in Fuling and will return in March 2012 to continue the work. Dr. Macfarlane is a frequent presenter at local, regional, and international conferences. She has also written several chapters on assessment and instructional practice along with other publications.

Greg Orlowsky
Greg is a highly valued member of the Instructional Technology team at Pacific University, widely know as the "Apple Guy," who solves many of our tech issues and invariably gives good advice to the Berglund Center.

Erin Murphy
Erin Murphy is the author of five collections of poetry: *Distant Glitter* (forthcoming from Word Press in 2013); *Word Problems* (Word Press, 2011); *Dislocation and Other Theories* (Word Press, 2008), winner of the Paterson Prize for Literary Excellence; *Too Much of This World* (Mammoth Books, 2008), winner of the Anthony Piccione Poetry Prize; and *Science of Desire* (Word Press, 2004), a finalist for the Paterson Poetry Prize for the best poetry book of 2004. With Todd Davis, she is co-editor of *Making Poems: 40 Poems with Commentary by the Poets* (State University of New York Press, 2010). Her awards include a $5,000 Dorothy Sargent Rosenberg Poetry Prize, the Foley Poetry Award, the National Writers' Union Poetry Award judged by Donald Hall, The Normal School Poetry Prize judged by Nick Flynn, and fellowships from the Pennsylvania Council on the Arts, the Maryland State Arts Council, and the Virginia Center for the Creative Arts. Her work has been featured on Garrison Keillor's *The Writer's Almanac*, and her poems and creative nonfiction essays have appeared in numerous journals and anthologies, including *180 More: Extraordinary Poems for Every Day*, edited by Billy Collins (Random House), *The Art of Losing*, edited by Kevin Young (Bloomsbury), and *The 2009 Best of the Net* anthology, judged by Patricia Smith. For her publications and outreach work in the literary arts, she was honored with the 2010 WISE Women of Blair County Tribute Award in Arts & Letters. She is associate professor of English and creative writing at the Pennsylvania State University, Altoona College, where she received the 2011 Alumni/Student Award for Excellence in Teaching. Website: http://www.erin-murphy.com

Nicole Nowlin, Berglund Student Fellow

Nicole is a graduate of Pacific University who has a degree Business Administration (International Business) and Japanese with a special interest in international relations. She was a Fulbright finalist for a research grant to Japan in 2011/2012 and was an active member of Pacific's Speech and Debate Team. In her spare time, she caters to her voracious appetite for fiction through novels, comics, movies, and writing. Her interest in comics, particularly Japanese manga, led her to her Student Fellowship in the Berglund Center for Internet Studies and her articles on scanlations and e-manga.

Robbie J. Pock, Assistant Teacher, Education

Robbie Pock is a graduate of Pacific University's MFA in Writing program, a teacher in Pacific's Learning Community, and an experienced online teacher. She has joined *Interface* as an editor in the field of On-Line Teaching. See her initial piece, "Cyber-School: The Challenges of Teaching and Learning Online From One English Instructor's perspective". Robbie effectively sums up the advantages and disadvantages of teaching online.

Steve Rhine, Ed. D.

Steve Rhine is a Professor of Education in the School of Education at Willamette University in Salem, Oregon. Dr. Rhine began as a high school mathematics teacher for eleven years. Upon completing his doctorate at UCLA, he began a career in teacher education that now spans 17 years. He has been awarded numerous federal and other grants focusing on uses of educational technology that total over $3.5 million. He directed the Oregon Technology in Education Network (OTEN), from 2001-04 that was then funded by the Preparing Tomorrow's Teachers to Use Technology (PT3) program. He has also been instrumental in a Teacher Quality Enhancement Partnership grant that funded OTEN 2004-09. He is currently working on a $740,000 Fund for the Improvement of Post-Secondary Education (FIPSE) grant that will make use of research on algebraic thinking to help prepare pre-service teachers with understanding of how students struggle as well as technological tools to help develop understanding of challenging topics in algebra. In 2000, he participated on the writing team for ISTE's National Educational Technology Standards (NETS) for Teachers. He has presented at multiple educational technology conferences. Dr. Rhine has taught courses in Educational Technology, Educational Psychology, Action Research, Multicultural Education, and Mathematics Education. His current research includes work on conducting online dialogue with student teachers based on digital video clips of their teaching, the role of Web 2.0 in classrooms, and the transition of Mexican and Ukrainian im/migrant students into Oregon schools. He has recently published two books. The first, "A Brilliant Teacher", an engaging account of his year-long trip around the world with his wife and three children. The second, "Integrated Technologies, Innovative Learning: Insights from the PT3 Program", an edited book of stories of efforts by institutions to integrate technology in the development of pre-service teachers.

Clare Richardson-Barlow, MA
Clare earned her BA from Pacific University in 2008 with a degree in Politics & Government and a minor in Chinese language. She received her MA in International Development and Public Policy from Tsinghua University in Beijing, China in 2010. Clare currently works in Washington, DC.

Mark Szymanski, Ph.D
Dr. Szymanski is a Professor in the College of Education with a background in technology and instruction, and cognitive science. He teaches Advanced Human Development and Psychology and Technology Across the Curriculum courses. He has been on the Editorial Board of *Interface* since it was founded in 2000. His research interests include the development of learning skills and environments informed by psychology and facilitated by technology. He's interested in project-based web 2.0 learning and the role of tablets in the classroom. He recently worked with a student, Doug Niel to develop an iPad App called Point Plotter for The Algebraic Thinking Project. His current scholarship includes:

Szymanski, M.J. (2011). *Pedagogical and Cognitive Frameworks for Interdisciplinary Learning with New Media.* A presentation given at the International Journal of Arts and Sciences Conference. Harvard University. Cambridge, MA.

Szymanski, M.J. (2011) Internet 2.0 and the Learning Sciences. The Untold Story of a Timely Meeting. *The Journal of Education, Community, and Values: Interface on the Internet, 9(2).*

Szymanski, M.J. & Wilkes, P. (2011).*Digital Depth and Complexity: Technology Integration Strategies for Differentiating Instruction with the Icons of Depth and Complexity.* 2011 California Association for the Gifted Conference, Palm Springs, CA.

Maria Walters

Maria Walters is a graduate of both Pacific University and the Berglund Center. In her roles as HTML Editor and Student Projects Manager between 2007 and 2009, she fell in love with the Internet as a whole and became excited to be a contributing part of it. After working at Intel for a year, she founded her own freelance writing business, specializing in writing for the web: Written to Be Read, LLC. Find out more about her business at http://www.writtentoberead.com. She blogs personally at http://rejournaling.me, recording the exploits of her younger self as recorded in her journals. She is currently a contract Instructional Designer and Trainer at Nike.

Index

A

Amazon, 6, 71, 72, 113, 114, 118, 120
Android, 104, 105
Apple, 29, 63, 65, 68, 123, 125, 207
application, 6, 119, 157, 173
    applications, 14, 15, 18, 23, 62, 72, 97, 105, 107, 155, 173, 203
    apps, 63, 64, 85, 104, 123, 124, 125, 201

B

Barnes and Noble, 6, 114
    Barnes & Noble, 8, 63, 72, 101, 103, 105, 107
Blackboard, 7, 1, 3, 4, 38
book, 3, 6, 10, 17, 30, 42, 61, 62, 64, 65, 68, 71, 72, 73, 104, 105, 106, 107, 110, 113, 117, 120, 133, 135, 136, 142, 148, 149, 151, 155, 157, 158, 161, 167, 168, 169, 193, 207, 209
    books, 14, 23, 41, 54, 64, 67, 68, 71, 72, 73, 103, 105, 106, 107, 109, 113, 114, 118, 120, 137, 140, 142, 143, 145, 148, 153, 167, 170, 173, 176, 178, 182, 204, 209
business, 5, 61, 64, 71, 75, 76, 79, 81, 85, 86, 97, 132, 142, 150, 168, 195, 196, 198, 200, 203, 204, 210

C

camera, 7, 125
child, 19, 72, 99
    children, 9, 54, 85, 149, 168, 206, 209
China, 5, 8, 105, 107, 113, 114, 129, 130, 131, 132, 133, 171, 183, 184, 186, 187, 188, 189, 190, 193, 194, 195, 196, 197, 198, 199, 200, 202, 203, 206, 209
    Chinese, 5, 8, 129, 130, 131, 132, 171, 173, 183, 184, 185, 186, 187, 188, 189, 190, 191, 193, 194, 196, 197, 199, 200, 201, 202, 203, 209
Christian, 133, 135, 161, 162, 164, 165, 167, 169
    Christianity, 162, 165
    Christians, 133, 135, 165
class, 4, 6, 7, 8, 9, 10, 23, 29, 32, 35, 37, 38, 39, 42, 123, 124, 146, 148, 201
classroom, 5, 6, 9, 13, 17, 20, 22, 31, 32, 33, 35, 36, 41, 42, 155, 158, 209
    classrooms, 14
cloud, 14, 110, 124, 173
    clouds, 14
communication, 9, 15, 27, 32, 38, 41, 42, 47, 48, 49, 89, 90, 91, 92, 93, 94, 96, 161, 163, 165, 195, 206
    communicate, 6, 7, 10, 90
    communicating, 93
computer, 5, 6, 8, 13, 20, 21, 23, 29, 31, 33, 72, 75, 89, 99, 109, 110, 113, 114, 124, 125, 149, 151, 152, 204
cyber, 10, 202
    cyberspace, 139, 199

D

data, 20, 27, 32, 33, 94, 109, 110, 132, 182, 202
digital, 7, 8, 1, 3, 26, 35, 59, 61, 62, 63, 64, 65, 66, 67, 69, 70, 71, 72, 73, 110, 127, 129, 135, 155, 156, 157, 158, 159, 161, 162, 165, 170, 199, 209
download, 4, 6, 8, 61, 64, 75, 105, 107, 110, 113, 114, 182, 195
    downloaded, 8, 105, 113, 114, 123
    downloading, 8, 77, 106, 107, 113, 114

E

economy, 130, 141, 169, 186
    economic, 41, 119, 129, 130, 132, 185, 186, 190, 193, 196, 198
    economics, 30, 186, 196
education, 7, 1, 3, 9, 13, 17, 18, 19, 21, 22, 23, 26, 29, 31, 32, 35, 36, 95, 124, 156, 157, 159, 201, 203, 204, 206, 208, 209
    educator, 15, 33, 155, 206
    educators, 15, 18, 21, 22, 36, 156, 158
electronic, 3, 6, 4, 5, 7, 8, 85, 113, 133, 135, 136, 161, 162, 190
email, 4, 7, 8, 18, 27, 42, 90, 91, 94, 95, 104, 105, 123, 141, 147, 163, 198
e-reader, 5
evangelical, 133, 135, 136
    evangelicals, 133, 134, 135, 136
    evangelism, 8, 127, 133, 161

F

Facebook, 7, 87, 89, 90, 91, 92, 93, 94, 95, 96, 97, 99, 104, 106, 140, 196
Flash, 14, 75, 76, 81, 104, 105, 125

G

Game, 7, 45, 53
    Gaming, 7, 45, 48
Google, 8, 13, 15, 93, 136, 148, 152, 163, 171, 173, 182, 194, 195
government, 130, 131, 132, 163, 178, 185, 187, 188, 189, 190, 196

H

health, 29

I

Interface, 3, 5, 6, 18, 19, 27, 42, 61, 121, 129, 137, 145, 202, 204, 206, 208, 209
Internet, 1, 3, 5, 6, 7, 8, 1, 3, 4, 5, 6, 8, 13, 14, 15, 17, 18, 19, 20, 21, 22, 23, 25, 27, 29, 30, 31, 32, 33, 37, 42, 43, 47, 75, 76, 77, 78, 79, 80, 96, 101, 103, 104, 109, 110, 111, 113, 114, 123, 127, 129, 130, 132, 133, 135, 137, 138, 139, 140, 141, 142, 143, 145, 146, 147, 148, 149, 150, 151, 152, 153, 156, 161, 163, 165, 167, 168, 169, 170, 171, 182, 183, 184, 188, 189, 194, 198, 199, 200, 202, 203, 205, 208, 209, 210
iPad, 8, 63, 64, 68, 71, 101, 103, 104, 107, 114, 123, 124, 125, 209
iPod, 63
  iPods, 14
iTunes, 6, 64, 124

J

Jesus, 8, 127, 134, 161, 162, 165

K

kid, 76, 77
  kids, 21, 41, 73, 85, 124, 157
Kindle, 8, 67, 68, 71, 72, 101, 103, 106, 107, 113, 114, 115, 120, 139, 140, 142, 143, 149, 151

L

law, 83, 188, 204
  laws, 7, 83, 85
learn, 6, 4, 5, 7, 13, 14, 15, 20, 27, 43, 51, 111, 123, 130, 133, 167, 174, 176, 182, 188, 201
  learning, 7, 1, 4, 9, 13, 15, 17, 20, 21, 22, 23, 24, 25, 35, 124, 158, 201, 203, 208, 209

M

Manga, 7, 59, 61, 62, 63, 64, 65, 66, 67, 68, 69, 70, 71, 72, 73
media, 7, 6, 55, 57, 59, 64, 65, 67, 68, 87, 90, 95, 117, 197, 205, 209
Microsoft, 6, 114, 132
mobile, 13, 36, 85
money, 30, 42, 62, 71, 76, 77, 78, 79, 97, 98, 110, 124
movies, 61, 64, 103, 113, 208
music, 23, 61, 75, 76, 77, 78, 79, 80, 103, 104, 134, 141, 150, 205
Myspace, 75, 76, 77

N

Netflix, 105, 107, 119, 120
network, 14, 20, 21, 90, 110, 163, 164, 169
  networked, 14, 20
  networking, 7, 31, 75, 77, 89, 90, 93, 94, 198
Nook, 8, 63, 67, 68, 71, 72, 103, 104, 105, 106, 107, 114

O

online, 6, 3, 4, 5, 7, 9, 10, 11, 17, 27, 31, 35, 37, 38, 39, 42, 47, 52, 62, 63, 64, 65, 66, 67, 68, 71, 72, 75, 77, 80, 85, 90, 91, 92, 93, 94, 95, 96, 97, 105, 106, 109, 110, 111, 113, 118, 120, 141, 151, 162, 163, 164, 165, 173, 193, 196, 198, 201, 204, 205, 206, 208

P

Pacific University, 3, 5, 6, 3, 9, 13, 17, 37, 41, 47, 48, 61, 69, 75, 89, 103, 109, 117, 123, 167, 203, 204, 205, 206, 207, 208, 209, 210
politics, 7, 83, 199, 209
  political, 41, 95, 96, 129, 132, 164, 183, 184, 185, 186, 187, 188, 190, 195, 196, 198
presentation, 4, 5, 6, 37, 90, 209
  presentations, 4, 6, 203
program, 21, 66, 67, 94, 104, 105, 106, 140, 201, 205, 206, 208
  programs, 4, 5, 6, 30, 104, 157, 159, 195
publish, 6, 21, 67
  publish, 21, 53, 54, 61, 71, 121, 137, 145, 149, 176, 178, 186, 194, 204, 209
  publisher, 3, 62, 63, 64, 65, 66, 67, 139
  publishing, 66, 142
publishing, 5, 22, 32, 61, 62, 63, 64, 65, 66, 67, 68, 69, 70, 71, 74, 78, 141, 142, 199

R

religion, 133, 136, 161, 193

S

scanlation, 61, 62, 66
School, 7, 1, 9, 19, 22, 23, 81, 89, 130, 204, 207, 208
SKYPE, 7, 1, 3, 6, 7, 8
Social, 7, 13, 14, 15, 25, 32, 41, 47, 49, 50, 51, 75, 77, 85, 87, 89, 90, 91, 92, 93, 94, 95, 96, 97, 98, 99, 140, 155, 158, 186, 188, 190, 203
stream, 48, 50, 71, 118, 125
  streaming, 7, 11, 19, 51, 64
student, 5, 6, 3, 4, 5, 6, 7, 8, 10, 18, 19, 20, 21, 22, 25, 27, 28, 32, 33, 36, 37, 38, 39, 41, 90, 104, 123, 124, 156, 159, 173, 174, 176, 178, 182, 189, 195, 196, 204, 206, 208, 209
  students, 6, 4, 5, 6, 7, 8, 9, 10, 11, 15, 17, 18, 19, 20, 21, 22, 23, 24, 26, 27, 29, 30, 31, 32, 33, 34, 35, 37, 38, 39, 42, 48, 90, 123, 142, 156, 157, 159, 189, 195, 202, 206, 208, 209

system, 3, 4, 5, 19, 20, 22, 26, 27, 29, 72, 78, 104, 105, 106, 107, 114, 117, 119, 124, 131, 132, 139, 183, 184, 186, 187, 188, 190

T

tablet, 5, 6
teacher, 7, 1, 3, 20, 26, 35, 208, 209
Technology, 8, 4, 5, 7, 17, 18, 21, 22, 23, 24, 25, 26, 27, 35, 36, 95, 101, 123, 129, 130, 156, 157, 159, 203, 207, 208, 209
telephone, 7, 41, 109
    iPhone, 70, 71, 104, 196, 201
textbook, 111
    textbooks, 4, 5, 29, 42, 123
travel, 110, 114, 115
    travelling, 68, 103
Twitter, 21, 48, 196, 200, 201

V

video, 7, 6, 45, 53

W

web, 8, 17, 18, 20, 21, 22, 23, 24, 28, 32, 61, 62, 63, 64, 65, 66, 67, 68, 69, 70, 71, 72, 73, 81, 95, 97, 117, 118, 119, 120, 121, 129, 133, 134, 136, 158, 161, 163, 171, 183, 203, 205, 208
    website, 7, 45, 47, 83, 85, 207
webinar, 5, 7
    webinars, 4, 5, 6, 7
website, 4, 24, 27, 31, 47, 50, 52, 67, 72, 85, 86, 89, 93, 104, 105, 163
    websites, 5, 8, 32, 75, 85
Windows, 6, 29

Y

Yahoo, 104
YouTube, 7, 15, 21, 104, 105

Made in United States
Troutdale, OR
11/03/2026

56852552R00124